BE STRONG
Lifestyle
JOURNAL

> "Courage is the most important of all the virtues because without courage, you can't practice any other virtue consistently."
>
> - MAYA ANGELOU -

CONTENTS

How to Use This Journal, 5

What is the Be Strong Lifestyle, 7

Brokenness vs. Wholeness, 8

Identifying My Brokenness, 9

Accountability Partners, 10

Stronger Days Calendar, 13

> "Strength and growth come only through continuous effort and struggle."
>
> - NAPOLEON HILL -

HOW TO USE THIS
JOURNAL

This journal is meant to trigger your thoughts in ways that confront your brokenness and deliver you to wholeness. In doing so, it contains inspirational quotes, integral explanations, recurrent questions, and frequent challenges. You are to write or even draw in the journal as your thoughts and ideas unfold. On some occasions, review what you have written as a means to sense your development. Whether you use a pencil or pen, write in full sentences or simple phrases, there is no wrong or right way to express yourself as it relates to this journal. There is only one goal: a better, stronger you!

The "Be Strong Lifestyle" moves people from being BROKEN to STRONG.

BROKEN LIFESTYLE → BE STRONG LIFESTYLE

Socially • Emotionally • Mentally • Physically • Spiritually

Socially • Emotionally • Mentally • Physically • Spiritually

Involves negative patterns from your family history or individual choices that are being repeated

Involves developing new patterns of thinking and behaving that reform your family or choices

WHAT IS THE BE STRONG LIFESTYLE?

The Be Strong Lifestyle is about being **comprehensive**, **courageous** and **consistent**.

Comprehensive means tackling all aspects of your life, not just your physical appearance, for instance. It means looking at yourself as a whole, integrated being wherein your emotions relate to your mental well-being as much as it does your physical self. In other words, all parts of you affect and impact the other parts. This includes your heart, mind, body, and spirit.

Being **courageous** is a significant part of the Be Strong Lifestyle because it involves change. We should be constantly seeking opportunities to grow and develop into better human beings that express this positive evolution for ourselves, our families and our communities. Being courageous means facing the truth of who we are, how we got this way and then what it takes to overcome the negative and accentuate the positive.

Being **consistent** is about responding differently on a regular basis to things that have triggered negative or unproductive patterns in our lives. Accomplishing this will require both a comprehensive look at our triggers, as well as the courage to address them. Basically, we have to form new, more positive habits through a holistic, fearless approach.

BROKENNESS vs. WHOLENESS

Brokenness shields you from the truth, allowing you to believe a misconception or lie that you now live with as the truth.

Broken people have allowed these lies to overcome them. Thus, they live as they were never meant, separated from their true essence and purpose. They are slaves to some destructive belief or feeling that causes them to act and react in unproductive ways, typically hurting themselves or those around them.

Wholeness doesn't mean you're perfect. It means you recognize and reject lies that once hindered you or could be hindering you from the truth of who you are. Will those lies keep trying to return and disrupt your life? Yes, but whole people know what tools to use and how to fight it.

IDENTIFYING MY BROKENNESS

What situation, person or group caused you to break? This could include things like a death, divorce, deception, abandonment, disappointment, and so forth.

What aspect of your life reflects this brokenness as a result? Are you:

Emotionally Imbalanced

Physically Diminished

Financially Irresponsible

Spiritually Disconnected

Mentally Confused

Socially Inept

ACCOUNTABILITY PARTNERS

While some people may need more help than others, everyone needs help at some point. This is especially true when you are tackling the confrontation of truth and the advent of change. As such, identifying people in our lives who can help us "keep it real" and "keep it moving," will ensure we can achieve the Be Strong Lifestyle at some level.

What person(s) or group can best help me be honest with myself about myself:

Emotionally _____

Mentally   _____

Physically   _____

Spiritually _____

Socially   _____

What person(s) or group can best help me be consistent with improving in these areas:

Emotionally _____

Mentally   _____

Physically   _____

Spiritually _____

Socially   _____

Contact these people or groups that you have listed above. Tell them what you're trying to achieve, and ask them to be your accountability partner to ensure you remain committed. Set up an interval or schedule when you ask them to contact you about your development.

"For what it's worth: It's never too late to be whoever you want to be. I hope you live a life you're proud of, and if you find you're not, I hope you have the strength to start over again."

- F. SCOTT FITZGERALD -

STRONGER DAYS

Because the first step to restoring your brokenness is admitting that you are broken, think about the aspect of your life that you most need to address this month:

_____

_____

_____

_____

_____

_____

_____

_____

For the next several weeks, think about how you can confront and overcome your issue(s) by writing down your thoughts on the following pages each day.

How do you feel about yourself and your life today?   **DATE:** _____

Emotionally   _____

Mentally   _____

Physically   _____

Spiritually   _____

Socially   _____

Courage Tools

What can I be thankful for?
Positivity _____

How do I say "stop," "no," "enough"?
Boundaries _____

Who do I need to forgive, including me?
Forgiveness _____

When or how can I confront this issue?
Confidence _____

What are the possibilities or opportunities?
Hope _____

Courage Challenge: What is something you can do or say differently today, which you have perhaps never done or done well before, that will challenge or change your broken pattern?

How do you feel about yourself and your life today?   **DATE:** _____

Emotionally   _____

Mentally   _____

Physically   _____

Spiritually   _____

Socially   _____

Courage Tools

What can I be thankful for?
Positivity _____

How do I say "stop," "no," "enough"?
Boundaries _____

Who do I need to forgive, including me?
Forgiveness _____

When or how can I confront this issue?
Confidence _____

What are the possibilities or opportunities?
Hope _____

Courage Challenge: What is something you can do or say differently today, which you have perhaps never done or done well before, that will challenge or change your broken pattern?

How do you feel about yourself and your life today? **DATE:** _____

Emotionally _____

Mentally _____

Physically _____

Spiritually _____

Socially _____

Courage Tools

What can I be thankful for?
Positivity _____

How do I say "stop," "no," "enough"?
Boundaries _____

Who do I need to forgive, including me?
Forgiveness _____

When or how can I confront this issue?
Confidence _____

What are the possibilities or opportunities?
Hope _____

Courage Challenge: What is something you can do or say differently today, which you have perhaps never done or done well before, that will challenge or change your broken pattern?

How do you feel about yourself and your life today?   **DATE:** _____

Emotionally _____

Mentally   _____

Physically   _____

Spiritually _____

Socially   _____

Courage Tools

What can I be thankful for?
Positivity _____

How do I say "stop," "no," "enough"?
Boundaries _____

Who do I need to forgive, including me?
Forgiveness _____

When or how can I confront this issue?
Confidence _____

What are the possibilities or opportunities?
Hope _____

Courage Challenge: What is something you can do or say differently today, which you have perhaps never done or done well before, that will challenge or change your broken pattern?

How do you feel about yourself and your life today? **DATE:** _____

Emotionally   _____

Mentally   _____

Physically   _____

Spiritually   _____

Socially   _____

Courage Tools

What can I be thankful for?
Positivity _____

How do I say "stop," "no," "enough"?
Boundaries _____

Who do I need to forgive, including me?
Forgiveness _____

When or how can I confront this issue?
Confidence _____

What are the possibilities or opportunities?
Hope _____

Courage Challenge: What is something you can do or say differently today, which you have perhaps never done or done well before, that will challenge or change your broken pattern?

How do you feel about yourself and your life today?   **DATE:** _____

Emotionally   _____

Mentally   _____

Physically   _____

Spiritually   _____

Socially   _____

Courage Tools

What can I be thankful for?
Positivity _____

How do I say "stop," "no," "enough"?
Boundaries _____

Who do I need to forgive, including me?
Forgiveness _____

When or how can I confront this issue?
Confidence _____

What are the possibilities or opportunities?
Hope _____

Courage Challenge: What is something you can do or say differently today, which you have perhaps never done or done well before, that will challenge or change your broken pattern?

How do you feel about yourself and your life today? **DATE:** _____

Emotionally _____

Mentally _____

Physically _____

Spiritually _____

Socially _____

Courage Tools

What can I be thankful for?
Positivity _____

How do I say "stop," "no," "enough"?
Boundaries _____

Who do I need to forgive, including me?
Forgiveness _____

When or how can I confront this issue?
Confidence _____

What are the possibilities or opportunities?
Hope _____

Courage Challenge: What is something you can do or say differently today, which you have perhaps never done or done well before, that will challenge or change your broken pattern?

Weekly
UPDATE..

From 1 to 10 with 10 being the best, how did you do this week with confronting, challenging or changing your broken patterns?

_____

Why did you do so well or so poorly?

_____

What is it going to take to get to the next level?

_____

How do you feel about yourself and your life today?   **DATE:** _____

Emotionally   _____

Mentally   _____

Physically   _____

Spiritually   _____

Socially   _____

Courage Tools

What can I be thankful for?
Positivity _____

How do I say "stop," "no," "enough"?
Boundaries _____

Who do I need to forgive, including me?
Forgiveness _____

When or how can I confront this issue?
Confidence _____

What are the possibilities or opportunities?
Hope _____

Courage Challenge: What is something you can do or say differently today, which you have perhaps never done or done well before, that will challenge or change your broken pattern?

How do you feel about yourself and your life today?   **DATE:** _____

Emotionally _____

Mentally _____

Physically _____

Spiritually _____

Socially _____

Courage Tools

What can I be thankful for?
Positivity _____

How do I say "stop," "no," "enough"?
Boundaries _____

Who do I need to forgive, including me?
Forgiveness _____

When or how can I confront this issue?
Confidence _____

What are the possibilities or opportunities?
Hope _____

Courage Challenge: What is something you can do or say differently today, which you have perhaps never done or done well before, that will challenge or change your broken pattern?

How do you feel about yourself and your life today? **DATE:** _____

Emotionally _____

Mentally _____

Physically _____

Spiritually _____

Socially _____

Courage Tools

What can I be thankful for?
Positivity _____

How do I say "stop," "no," "enough"?
Boundaries _____

Who do I need to forgive, including me?
Forgiveness _____

When or how can I confront this issue?
Confidence _____

What are the possibilities or opportunities?
Hope _____

Courage Challenge: What is something you can do or say differently today, which you have perhaps never done or done well before, that will challenge or change your broken pattern?

How do you feel about yourself and your life today?   **DATE:** _____

Emotionally   _____

Mentally   _____

Physically   _____

Spiritually   _____

Socially   _____

Courage Tools

What can I be thankful for?
Positivity _____

How do I say "stop," "no," "enough"?
Boundaries _____

Who do I need to forgive, including me?
Forgiveness _____

When or how can I confront this issue?
Confidence _____

What are the possibilities or opportunities?
Hope _____

Courage Challenge: What is something you can do or say differently today, which you have perhaps never done or done well before, that will challenge or change your broken pattern?

How do you feel about yourself and your life today?   **DATE:** _____

Emotionally   _____

Mentally   _____

Physically   _____

Spiritually   _____

Socially   _____

Courage Tools

What can I be thankful for?
Positivity _____

How do I say "stop," "no," "enough"?
Boundaries _____

Who do I need to forgive, including me?
Forgiveness _____

When or how can I confront this issue?
Confidence _____

What are the possibilities or opportunities?
Hope _____

Courage Challenge: What is something you can do or say differently today, which you have perhaps never done or done well before, that will challenge or change your broken pattern?

How do you feel about yourself and your life today?   **DATE:** _____

Emotionally _____

Mentally _____

Physically _____

Spiritually _____

Socially _____

Courage Tools

What can I be thankful for?
Positivity _____

How do I say "stop," "no," "enough"?
Boundaries _____

Who do I need to forgive, including me?
Forgiveness _____

When or how can I confront this issue?
Confidence _____

What are the possibilities or opportunities?
Hope _____

Courage Challenge: What is something you can do or say differently today, which you have perhaps never done or done well before, that will challenge or change your broken pattern?

How do you feel about yourself and your life today? **DATE:** _____

Emotionally _____

Mentally _____

Physically _____

Spiritually _____

Socially _____

Courage Tools

What can I be thankful for?
Positivity _____

How do I say "stop," "no," "enough"?
Boundaries _____

Who do I need to forgive, including me?
Forgiveness _____

When or how can I confront this issue?
Confidence _____

What are the possibilities or opportunities?
Hope _____

Courage Challenge: What is something you can do or say differently today, which you have perhaps never done or done well before, that will challenge or change your broken pattern?

Weekly
U P D A T E . .

From 1 to 10 with 10 being the best, how did you do this week with confronting, challenging or changing your broken patterns?

_____

Why did you do so well or so poorly?

_____

What is it going to take to get to the next level?

_____

How do you feel about yourself and your life today?   **DATE:** _____

Emotionally _____

Mentally _____

Physically _____

Spiritually _____

Socially _____

Courage Tools

What can I be thankful for?
Positivity _____

How do I say "stop," "no," "enough"?
Boundaries _____

Who do I need to forgive, including me?
Forgiveness _____

When or how can I confront this issue?
Confidence _____

What are the possibilities or opportunities?
Hope _____

Courage Challenge: What is something you can do or say differently today, which you have perhaps never done or done well before, that will challenge or change your broken pattern?

How do you feel about yourself and your life today?   **DATE:** _____

Emotionally   _____

Mentally   _____

Physically   _____

Spiritually   _____

Socially   _____

Courage Tools

What can I be thankful for?
Positivity _____

How do I say "stop," "no," "enough"?
Boundaries _____

Who do I need to forgive, including me?
Forgiveness _____

When or how can I confront this issue?
Confidence _____

What are the possibilities or opportunities?
Hope _____

Courage Challenge: What is something you can do or say differently today, which you have perhaps never done or done well before, that will challenge or change your broken pattern?

How do you feel about yourself and your life today? **DATE:** _____

Emotionally _____

Mentally _____

Physically _____

Spiritually _____

Socially _____

Courage Tools

What can I be thankful for?
Positivity _____

How do I say "stop," "no," "enough"?
Boundaries _____

Who do I need to forgive, including me?
Forgiveness _____

When or how can I confront this issue?
Confidence _____

What are the possibilities or opportunities?
Hope _____

Courage Challenge: What is something you can do or say differently today, which you have perhaps never done or done well before, that will challenge or change your broken pattern?

How do you feel about yourself and your life today? **DATE:** _____

Emotionally _____

Mentally _____

Physically _____

Spiritually _____

Socially _____

Courage Tools

What can I be thankful for?
Positivity _____

How do I say "stop," "no," "enough"?
Boundaries _____

Who do I need to forgive, including me?
Forgiveness _____

When or how can I confront this issue?
Confidence _____

What are the possibilities or opportunities?
Hope _____

Courage Challenge: What is something you can do or say differently today, which you have perhaps never done or done well before, that will challenge or change your broken pattern?

How do you feel about yourself and your life today?   **DATE:** _____

Emotionally   _____

Mentally   _____

Physically   _____

Spiritually   _____

Socially   _____

Courage Tools

What can I be thankful for?
Positivity _____

How do I say "stop," "no," "enough"?
Boundaries _____

Who do I need to forgive, including me?
Forgiveness _____

When or how can I confront this issue?
Confidence _____

What are the possibilities or opportunities?
Hope _____

Courage Challenge: What is something you can do or say differently today, which you have perhaps never done or done well before, that will challenge or change your broken pattern?

How do you feel about yourself and your life today?   **DATE:** _____

Emotionally _____

Mentally _____

Physically _____

Spiritually _____

Socially _____

Courage Tools

What can I be thankful for?
Positivity _____

How do I say "stop," "no," "enough"?
Boundaries _____

Who do I need to forgive, including me?
Forgiveness _____

When or how can I confront this issue?
Confidence _____

What are the possibilities or opportunities?
Hope _____

Courage Challenge: What is something you can do or say differently today, which you have perhaps never done or done well before, that will challenge or change your broken pattern?

How do you feel about yourself and your life today? **DATE:** _____

Emotionally _____

Mentally _____

Physically _____

Spiritually _____

Socially _____

Courage Tools

What can I be thankful for?
Positivity _____

How do I say "stop," "no," "enough"?
Boundaries _____

Who do I need to forgive, including me?
Forgiveness _____

When or how can I confront this issue?
Confidence _____

What are the possibilities or opportunities?
Hope _____

Courage Challenge: What is something you can do or say differently today, which you have perhaps never done or done well before, that will challenge or change your broken pattern?

Weekly
U P D A T E . .

From 1 to 10 with 10 being the best, how did you do this week with confronting, challenging or changing your broken patterns?

_____

Why did you do so well or so poorly?

_____

What is it going to take to get to the next level?

_____

How do you feel about yourself and your life today? **DATE:** _____

Emotionally _____

Mentally _____

Physically _____

Spiritually _____

Socially _____

Courage Tools

What can I be thankful for?
Positivity _____

How do I say "stop," "no," "enough"?
Boundaries _____

Who do I need to forgive, including me?
Forgiveness _____

When or how can I confront this issue?
Confidence _____

What are the possibilities or opportunities?
Hope _____

Courage Challenge: What is something you can do or say differently today, which you have perhaps never done or done well before, that will challenge or change your broken pattern?

How do you feel about yourself and your life today?   **DATE:** _____

Emotionally   _____

Mentally   _____

Physically   _____

Spiritually   _____

Socially   _____

Courage Tools

What can I be thankful for?
Positivity _____

How do I say "stop," "no," "enough"?
Boundaries _____

Who do I need to forgive, including me?
Forgiveness _____

When or how can I confront this issue?
Confidence _____

What are the possibilities or opportunities?
Hope _____

Courage Challenge: What is something you can do or say differently today, which you have perhaps never done or done well before, that will challenge or change your broken pattern?

How do you feel about yourself and your life today?   **DATE:** _____

Emotionally   _____

Mentally   _____

Physically   _____

Spiritually   _____

Socially   _____

Courage Tools

What can I be thankful for?
Positivity _____

How do I say "stop," "no," "enough"?
Boundaries _____

Who do I need to forgive, including me?
Forgiveness _____

When or how can I confront this issue?
Confidence _____

What are the possibilities or opportunities?
Hope _____

Courage Challenge: What is something you can do or say differently today, which you have perhaps never done or done well before, that will challenge or change your broken pattern?

How do you feel about yourself and your life today?   **DATE:** _____

Emotionally   _____

Mentally   _____

Physically   _____

Spiritually   _____

Socially   _____

Courage Tools

What can I be thankful for?
Positivity _____

How do I say "stop," "no," "enough"?
Boundaries _____

Who do I need to forgive, including me?
Forgiveness _____

When or how can I confront this issue?
Confidence _____

What are the possibilities or opportunities?
Hope _____

Courage Challenge: What is something you can do or say differently today, which you have perhaps never done or done well before, that will challenge or change your broken pattern?

How do you feel about yourself and your life today? **DATE:** _____

Emotionally _____

Mentally _____

Physically _____

Spiritually _____

Socially _____

Courage Tools

What can I be thankful for?
Positivity _____

How do I say "stop," "no," "enough"?
Boundaries _____

Who do I need to forgive, including me?
Forgiveness _____

When or how can I confront this issue?
Confidence _____

What are the possibilities or opportunities?
Hope _____

Courage Challenge: What is something you can do or say differently today, which you have perhaps never done or done well before, that will challenge or change your broken pattern?

How do you feel about yourself and your life today? **DATE:** _____

Emotionally _____

Mentally _____

Physically _____

Spiritually _____

Socially _____

Courage Tools

What can I be thankful for?
Positivity _____

How do I say "stop," "no," "enough"?
Boundaries _____

Who do I need to forgive, including me?
Forgiveness _____

When or how can I confront this issue?
Confidence _____

What are the possibilities or opportunities?
Hope _____

Courage Challenge: What is something you can do or say differently today, which you have perhaps never done or done well before, that will challenge or change your broken pattern?

How do you feel about yourself and your life today? **DATE:** _____

Emotionally _____

Mentally _____

Physically _____

Spiritually _____

Socially _____

Courage Tools

What can I be thankful for?
Positivity _____

How do I say "stop," "no," "enough"?
Boundaries _____

Who do I need to forgive, including me?
Forgiveness _____

When or how can I confront this issue?
Confidence _____

What are the possibilities or opportunities?
Hope _____

Courage Challenge: What is something you can do or say differently today, which you have perhaps never done or done well before, that will challenge or change your broken pattern?

Weekly
U P D A T E . .

From 1 to 10 with 10 being the best, how did you do this week with confronting, challenging or changing your broken patterns?

_____

Why did you do so well or so poorly?

_____

What is it going to take to get to the next level?

_____

"With the new day comes new strength and new thoughts."

- ELEANOR ROOSEVELT -

STRONGER DAYS

Because the first step to restoring your brokenness is admitting that you are broken, think about the aspect of your life that you most need to address this month:

_____

_____

_____

_____

_____

_____

_____

For the next several weeks, think about how you can confront and overcome your issue(s) by writing down your thoughts on the following pages each day.

How do you feel about yourself and your life today?   **DATE:** _____

Emotionally _____

Mentally _____

Physically _____

Spiritually _____

Socially _____

Courage Tools

What can I be thankful for?
Positivity _____

How do I say "stop," "no," "enough"?
Boundaries _____

Who do I need to forgive, including me?
Forgiveness _____

When or how can I confront this issue?
Confidence _____

What are the possibilities or opportunities?
Hope _____

Courage Challenge: What is something you can do or say differently today, which you have perhaps never done or done well before, that will challenge or change your broken pattern?

How do you feel about yourself and your life today?   **DATE:** _____

Emotionally   _____

Mentally   _____

Physically   _____

Spiritually   _____

Socially   _____

Courage Tools

What can I be thankful for?
Positivity _____

How do I say "stop," "no," "enough"?
Boundaries _____

Who do I need to forgive, including me?
Forgiveness _____

When or how can I confront this issue?
Confidence _____

What are the possibilities or opportunities?
Hope _____

Courage Challenge: What is something you can do or say differently today, which you have perhaps never done or done well before, that will challenge or change your broken pattern?

How do you feel about yourself and your life today?   **DATE:** _____

Emotionally _____

Mentally   _____

Physically   _____

Spiritually _____

Socially   _____

Courage Tools

What can I be thankful for?
Positivity _____

How do I say "stop," "no," "enough"?
Boundaries _____

Who do I need to forgive, including me?
Forgiveness _____

When or how can I confront this issue?
Confidence _____

What are the possibilities or opportunities?
Hope _____

Courage Challenge: What is something you can do or say differently today, which you have perhaps never done or done well before, that will challenge or change your broken pattern?

How do you feel about yourself and your life today? **DATE:** _____

Emotionally _____
Mentally _____
Physically _____
Spiritually _____
Socially _____

Courage Tools

What can I be thankful for?
Positivity _____

How do I say "stop," "no," "enough"?
Boundaries _____

Who do I need to forgive, including me?
Forgiveness _____

When or how can I confront this issue?
Confidence _____

What are the possibilities or opportunities?
Hope _____

Courage Challenge: What is something you can do or say differently today, which you have perhaps never done or done well before, that will challenge or change your broken pattern?

How do you feel about yourself and your life today?   **DATE:** _____

Emotionally   _____

Mentally   _____

Physically   _____

Spiritually   _____

Socially   _____

Courage Tools

What can I be thankful for?
Positivity _____

How do I say "stop," "no," "enough"?
Boundaries _____

Who do I need to forgive, including me?
Forgiveness _____

When or how can I confront this issue?
Confidence _____

What are the possibilities or opportunities?
Hope _____

Courage Challenge: What is something you can do or say differently today, which you have perhaps never done or done well before, that will challenge or change your broken pattern?

How do you feel about yourself and your life today?   **DATE:** _____

Emotionally _____

Mentally   _____

Physically   _____

Spiritually _____

Socially   _____

Courage Tools

What can I be thankful for?
Positivity _____

How do I say "stop," "no," "enough"?
Boundaries _____

Who do I need to forgive, including me?
Forgiveness _____

When or how can I confront this issue?
Confidence _____

What are the possibilities or opportunities?
Hope _____

Courage Challenge: What is something you can do or say differently today, which you have perhaps never done or done well before, that will challenge or change your broken pattern?

How do you feel about yourself and your life today?   **DATE:** _____

Emotionally   _____

Mentally   _____

Physically   _____

Spiritually   _____

Socially   _____

Courage Tools

What can I be thankful for?
Positivity _____

How do I say "stop," "no," "enough"?
Boundaries _____

Who do I need to forgive, including me?
Forgiveness _____

When or how can I confront this issue?
Confidence _____

What are the possibilities or opportunities?
Hope _____

Courage Challenge: What is something you can do or say differently today, which you have perhaps never done or done well before, that will challenge or change your broken pattern?

From 1 to 10 with 10 being the best, how did you do this week with confronting, challenging or changing your broken patterns?

_____

Why did you do so well or so poorly?

_____

What is it going to take to get to the next level?

_____

How do you feel about yourself and your life today? **DATE:** _____

Emotionally _____

Mentally _____

Physically _____

Spiritually _____

Socially _____

Courage Tools

What can I be thankful for?
Positivity _____

How do I say "stop," "no," "enough"?
Boundaries _____

Who do I need to forgive, including me?
Forgiveness _____

When or how can I confront this issue?
Confidence _____

What are the possibilities or opportunities?
Hope _____

Courage Challenge: What is something you can do or say differently today, which you have perhaps never done or done well before, that will challenge or change your broken pattern?

How do you feel about yourself and your life today? **DATE:** _____

Emotionally _____

Mentally _____

Physically _____

Spiritually _____

Socially _____

Courage Tools

What can I be thankful for?
Positivity _____

How do I say "stop," "no," "enough"?
Boundaries _____

Who do I need to forgive, including me?
Forgiveness _____

When or how can I confront this issue?
Confidence _____

What are the possibilities or opportunities?
Hope _____

Courage Challenge: What is something you can do or say differently today, which you have perhaps never done or done well before, that will challenge or change your broken pattern?

How do you feel about yourself and your life today?   **DATE:** _____

Emotionally   _____

Mentally   _____

Physically   _____

Spiritually   _____

Socially   _____

Courage Tools

What can I be thankful for?
Positivity _____

How do I say "stop," "no," "enough"?
Boundaries _____

Who do I need to forgive, including me?
Forgiveness _____

When or how can I confront this issue?
Confidence _____

What are the possibilities or opportunities?
Hope _____

Courage Challenge: What is something you can do or say differently today, which you have perhaps never done or done well before, that will challenge or change your broken pattern?

How do you feel about yourself and your life today?   **DATE:** _____

Emotionally   _____

Mentally   _____

Physically   _____

Spiritually   _____

Socially   _____

Courage Tools

What can I be thankful for?
Positivity _____

How do I say "stop," "no," "enough"?
Boundaries _____

Who do I need to forgive, including me?
Forgiveness _____

When or how can I confront this issue?
Confidence _____

What are the possibilities or opportunities?
Hope _____

Courage Challenge: What is something you can do or say differently today, which you have perhaps never done or done well before, that will challenge or change your broken pattern?

How do you feel about yourself and your life today?   **DATE:** _____

Emotionally _____

Mentally _____

Physically _____

Spiritually _____

Socially _____

Courage Tools

What can I be thankful for?
Positivity _____

How do I say "stop," "no," "enough"?
Boundaries _____

Who do I need to forgive, including me?
Forgiveness _____

When or how can I confront this issue?
Confidence _____

What are the possibilities or opportunities?
Hope _____

Courage Challenge: What is something you can do or say differently today, which you have perhaps never done or done well before, that will challenge or change your broken pattern?

How do you feel about yourself and your life today?   **DATE:** _____

Emotionally   _____

Mentally   _____

Physically   _____

Spiritually   _____

Socially   _____

Courage Tools

What can I be thankful for?
Positivity _____

How do I say "stop," "no," "enough"?
Boundaries _____

Who do I need to forgive, including me?
Forgiveness _____

When or how can I confront this issue?
Confidence _____

What are the possibilities or opportunities?
Hope _____

Courage Challenge: What is something you can do or say differently today, which you have perhaps never done or done well before, that will challenge or change your broken pattern?

How do you feel about yourself and your life today?   **DATE:** _____

Emotionally _____

Mentally _____

Physically _____

Spiritually _____

Socially _____

Courage Tools

What can I be thankful for?
Positivity _____

How do I say "stop," "no," "enough"?
Boundaries _____

Who do I need to forgive, including me?
Forgiveness _____

When or how can I confront this issue?
Confidence _____

What are the possibilities or opportunities?
Hope _____

Courage Challenge: What is something you can do or say differently today, which you have perhaps never done or done well before, that will challenge or change your broken pattern?

Weekly
U P D A T E . .

From 1 to 10 with 10 being the best, how did you do this week with confronting, challenging or changing your broken patterns?

_____

Why did you do so well or so poorly?

_____

What is it going to take to get to the next level?

_____

How do you feel about yourself and your life today? **DATE:** _____

Emotionally _____

Mentally _____

Physically _____

Spiritually _____

Socially _____

Courage Tools

What can I be thankful for?
Positivity _____

How do I say "stop," "no," "enough"?
Boundaries _____

Who do I need to forgive, including me?
Forgiveness _____

When or how can I confront this issue?
Confidence _____

What are the possibilities or opportunities?
Hope _____

Courage Challenge: What is something you can do or say differently today, which you have perhaps never done or done well before, that will challenge or change your broken pattern?

How do you feel about yourself and your life today?　**DATE:**

Emotionally _____

Mentally _____

Physically _____

Spiritually _____

Socially _____

Courage Tools

What can I be thankful for?
Positivity _____

How do I say "stop," "no," "enough"?
Boundaries _____

Who do I need to forgive, including me?
Forgiveness _____

When or how can I confront this issue?
Confidence _____

What are the possibilities or opportunities?
Hope _____

Courage Challenge: What is something you can do or say differently today, which you have perhaps never done or done well before, that will challenge or change your broken pattern?

How do you feel about yourself and your life today?   **DATE:** _____

Emotionally _____
Mentally   _____
Physically   _____
Spiritually _____
Socially   _____

Courage Tools

What can I be thankful for?
Positivity _____

How do I say "stop," "no," "enough"?
Boundaries _____

Who do I need to forgive, including me?
Forgiveness _____

When or how can I confront this issue?
Confidence _____

What are the possibilities or opportunities?
Hope _____

Courage Challenge: What is something you can do or say differently today, which you have perhaps never done or done well before, that will challenge or change your broken pattern?

How do you feel about yourself and your life today? **DATE:** _____

Emotionally _____

Mentally _____

Physically _____

Spiritually _____

Socially _____

Courage Tools

What can I be thankful for?
Positivity _____

How do I say "stop," "no," "enough"?
Boundaries _____

Who do I need to forgive, including me?
Forgiveness _____

When or how can I confront this issue?
Confidence _____

What are the possibilities or opportunities?
Hope _____

Courage Challenge: What is something you can do or say differently today, which you have perhaps never done or done well before, that will challenge or change your broken pattern?

How do you feel about yourself and your life today? **DATE:** _____

Emotionally _____

Mentally _____

Physically _____

Spiritually _____

Socially _____

Courage Tools

What can I be thankful for?
Positivity _____

How do I say "stop," "no," "enough"?
Boundaries _____

Who do I need to forgive, including me?
Forgiveness _____

When or how can I confront this issue?
Confidence _____

What are the possibilities or opportunities?
Hope _____

Courage Challenge: What is something you can do or say differently today, which you have perhaps never done or done well before, that will challenge or change your broken pattern?

How do you feel about yourself and your life today?　　**DATE:** _____

Emotionally　_____

Mentally　_____

Physically　_____

Spiritually　_____

Socially　_____

Courage Tools

What can I be thankful for?
Positivity _____

How do I say "stop," "no," "enough"?
Boundaries _____

Who do I need to forgive, including me?
Forgiveness _____

When or how can I confront this issue?
Confidence _____

What are the possibilities or opportunities?
Hope _____

Courage Challenge: What is something you can do or say differently today, which you have perhaps never done or done well before, that will challenge or change your broken pattern?

How do you feel about yourself and your life today?   **DATE:** _____

Emotionally   _____

Mentally   _____

Physically   _____

Spiritually   _____

Socially   _____

Courage Tools

What can I be thankful for?
Positivity _____

How do I say "stop," "no," "enough"?
Boundaries _____

Who do I need to forgive, including me?
Forgiveness _____

When or how can I confront this issue?
Confidence _____

What are the possibilities or opportunities?
Hope _____

Courage Challenge: What is something you can do or say differently today, which you have perhaps never done or done well before, that will challenge or change your broken pattern?

Weekly
U P D A T E . .

From 1 to 10 with 10 being the best, how did you do this week with confronting, challenging or changing your broken patterns?

_____

Why did you do so well or so poorly?

_____

What is it going to take to get to the next level?

_____

How do you feel about yourself and your life today? **DATE:** _____

Emotionally _____

Mentally _____

Physically _____

Spiritually _____

Socially _____

Courage Tools

What can I be thankful for?
Positivity _____

How do I say "stop," "no," "enough"?
Boundaries _____

Who do I need to forgive, including me?
Forgiveness _____

When or how can I confront this issue?
Confidence _____

What are the possibilities or opportunities?
Hope _____

Courage Challenge: What is something you can do or say differently today, which you have perhaps never done or done well before, that will challenge or change your broken pattern?

How do you feel about yourself and your life today?   **DATE:** _____

Emotionally   _____

Mentally   _____

Physically   _____

Spiritually   _____

Socially   _____

Courage Tools

What can I be thankful for?
Positivity _____

How do I say "stop," "no," "enough"?
Boundaries _____

Who do I need to forgive, including me?
Forgiveness _____

When or how can I confront this issue?
Confidence _____

What are the possibilities or opportunities?
Hope _____

Courage Challenge: What is something you can do or say differently today, which you have perhaps never done or done well before, that will challenge or change your broken pattern?

How do you feel about yourself and your life today?   **DATE:** _____

Emotionally _____

Mentally   _____

Physically   _____

Spiritually _____

Socially   _____

Courage Tools

What can I be thankful for?
Positivity _____

How do I say "stop," "no," "enough"?
Boundaries _____

Who do I need to forgive, including me?
Forgiveness _____

When or how can I confront this issue?
Confidence _____

What are the possibilities or opportunities?
Hope _____

Courage Challenge: What is something you can do or say differently today, which you have perhaps never done or done well before, that will challenge or change your broken pattern?

How do you feel about yourself and your life today?   **DATE:** _____

Emotionally _____

Mentally _____

Physically _____

Spiritually _____

Socially _____

Courage Tools

What can I be thankful for?
Positivity _____

How do I say "stop," "no," "enough"?
Boundaries _____

Who do I need to forgive, including me?
Forgiveness _____

When or how can I confront this issue?
Confidence _____

What are the possibilities or opportunities?
Hope _____

Courage Challenge: What is something you can do or say differently today, which you have perhaps never done or done well before, that will challenge or change your broken pattern?

How do you feel about yourself and your life today? **DATE:** _____

Emotionally _____

Mentally _____

Physically _____

Spiritually _____

Socially _____

Courage Tools

What can I be thankful for?
Positivity _____

How do I say "stop," "no," "enough"?
Boundaries _____

Who do I need to forgive, including me?
Forgiveness _____

When or how can I confront this issue?
Confidence _____

What are the possibilities or opportunities?
Hope _____

Courage Challenge: What is something you can do or say differently today, which you have perhaps never done or done well before, that will challenge or change your broken pattern?

How do you feel about yourself and your life today? **DATE:** _____

Emotionally _____

Mentally _____

Physically _____

Spiritually _____

Socially _____

Courage Tools

What can I be thankful for?
Positivity _____

How do I say "stop," "no," "enough"?
Boundaries _____

Who do I need to forgive, including me?
Forgiveness _____

When or how can I confront this issue?
Confidence _____

What are the possibilities or opportunities?
Hope _____

Courage Challenge: What is something you can do or say differently today, which you have perhaps never done or done well before, that will challenge or change your broken pattern?

How do you feel about yourself and your life today? **DATE:** _____

Emotionally _____

Mentally _____

Physically _____

Spiritually _____

Socially _____

Courage Tools

What can I be thankful for?
Positivity _____

How do I say "stop," "no," "enough"?
Boundaries _____

Who do I need to forgive, including me?
Forgiveness _____

When or how can I confront this issue?
Confidence _____

What are the possibilities or opportunities?
Hope _____

Courage Challenge: What is something you can do or say differently today, which you have perhaps never done or done well before, that will challenge or change your broken pattern?

Weekly
U P D A T E . .

From 1 to 10 with 10 being the best, how did you do this week with confronting, challenging or changing your broken patterns?

_____

Why did you do so well or so poorly?

_____

What is it going to take to get to the next level?

_____

> "Calm mind brings inner strength and self-confidence, so that's very important for good health."

— DALAI LAMA —

STRONGER DAYS

Because the first step to restoring your brokenness is admitting that you are broken, think about the aspect of your life that you most need to address this month:

_____

_____

_____

_____

_____

_____

_____

For the next several weeks, think about how you can confront and overcome your issue(s) by writing down your thoughts on the following pages each day.

How do you feel about yourself and your life today?   **DATE:** _____

Emotionally _____

Mentally   _____

Physically   _____

Spiritually _____

Socially   _____

Courage Tools

What can I be thankful for?
Positivity _____

How do I say "stop," "no," "enough"?
Boundaries _____

Who do I need to forgive, including me?
Forgiveness _____

When or how can I confront this issue?
Confidence _____

What are the possibilities or opportunities?
Hope _____

Courage Challenge: What is something you can do or say differently today, which you have perhaps never done or done well before, that will challenge or change your broken pattern?

How do you feel about yourself and your life today? **DATE:** _____

Emotionally _____

Mentally _____

Physically _____

Spiritually _____

Socially _____

Courage Tools

What can I be thankful for?
Positivity _____

How do I say "stop," "no," "enough"?
Boundaries _____

Who do I need to forgive, including me?
Forgiveness _____

When or how can I confront this issue?
Confidence _____

What are the possibilities or opportunities?
Hope _____

Courage Challenge: What is something you can do or say differently today, which you have perhaps never done or done well before, that will challenge or change your broken pattern?

How do you feel about yourself and your life today?   **DATE:** _____

Emotionally _____

Mentally _____

Physically _____

Spiritually _____

Socially _____

Courage Tools

What can I be thankful for?
Positivity _____

How do I say "stop," "no," "enough"?
Boundaries _____

Who do I need to forgive, including me?
Forgiveness _____

When or how can I confront this issue?
Confidence _____

What are the possibilities or opportunities?
Hope _____

Courage Challenge: What is something you can do or say differently today, which you have perhaps never done or done well before, that will challenge or change your broken pattern?

How do you feel about yourself and your life today? **DATE:** _____

Emotionally _____

Mentally _____

Physically _____

Spiritually _____

Socially _____

Courage Tools

What can I be thankful for?
Positivity _____

How do I say "stop," "no," "enough"?
Boundaries _____

Who do I need to forgive, including me?
Forgiveness _____

When or how can I confront this issue?
Confidence _____

What are the possibilities or opportunities?
Hope _____

Courage Challenge: What is something you can do or say differently today, which you have perhaps never done or done well before, that will challenge or change your broken pattern?

How do you feel about yourself and your life today?   **DATE:** _____

Emotionally _____

Mentally _____

Physically _____

Spiritually _____

Socially _____

Courage Tools

What can I be thankful for?
Positivity _____

How do I say "stop," "no," "enough"?
Boundaries _____

Who do I need to forgive, including me?
Forgiveness _____

When or how can I confront this issue?
Confidence _____

What are the possibilities or opportunities?
Hope _____

Courage Challenge: What is something you can do or say differently today, which you have perhaps never done or done well before, that will challenge or change your broken pattern?

How do you feel about yourself and your life today?   **DATE:** _____

Emotionally   _____

Mentally   _____

Physically   _____

Spiritually   _____

Socially   _____

Courage Tools

What can I be thankful for?
Positivity _____

How do I say "stop," "no," "enough"?
Boundaries _____

Who do I need to forgive, including me?
Forgiveness _____

When or how can I confront this issue?
Confidence _____

What are the possibilities or opportunities?
Hope _____

Courage Challenge: What is something you can do or say differently today, which you have perhaps never done or done well before, that will challenge or change your broken pattern?

How do you feel about yourself and your life today?   **DATE:** _____

Emotionally   _____

Mentally   _____

Physically   _____

Spiritually   _____

Socially   _____

Courage Tools

What can I be thankful for?
Positivity _____

How do I say "stop," "no," "enough"?
Boundaries _____

Who do I need to forgive, including me?
Forgiveness _____

When or how can I confront this issue?
Confidence _____

What are the possibilities or opportunities?
Hope _____

Courage Challenge: What is something you can do or say differently today, which you have perhaps never done or done well before, that will challenge or change your broken pattern?

Weekly
U P D A T E . .

From 1 to 10 with 10 being the best, how did you do this week with confronting, challenging or changing your broken patterns?

_____

Why did you do so well or so poorly?

_____

What is it going to take to get to the next level?

_____

How do you feel about yourself and your life today?   **DATE:** _____

Emotionally _____

Mentally _____

Physically _____

Spiritually _____

Socially _____

Courage Tools

What can I be thankful for?
Positivity _____

How do I say "stop," "no," "enough"?
Boundaries _____

Who do I need to forgive, including me?
Forgiveness _____

When or how can I confront this issue?
Confidence _____

What are the possibilities or opportunities?
Hope _____

Courage Challenge: What is something you can do or say differently today, which you have perhaps never done or done well before, that will challenge or change your broken pattern?

How do you feel about yourself and your life today?   **DATE:** _____

Emotionally   _____

Mentally   _____

Physically   _____

Spiritually   _____

Socially   _____

Courage Tools

What can I be thankful for?
Positivity _____

How do I say "stop," "no," "enough"?
Boundaries _____

Who do I need to forgive, including me?
Forgiveness _____

When or how can I confront this issue?
Confidence _____

What are the possibilities or opportunities?
Hope _____

Courage Challenge: What is something you can do or say differently today, which you have perhaps never done or done well before, that will challenge or change your broken pattern?

How do you feel about yourself and your life today? **DATE:** _____

Emotionally _____

Mentally _____

Physically _____

Spiritually _____

Socially _____

Courage Tools

What can I be thankful for?
Positivity _____

How do I say "stop," "no," "enough"?
Boundaries _____

Who do I need to forgive, including me?
Forgiveness _____

When or how can I confront this issue?
Confidence _____

What are the possibilities or opportunities?
Hope _____

Courage Challenge: What is something you can do or say differently today, which you have perhaps never done or done well before, that will challenge or change your broken pattern?

How do you feel about yourself and your life today? **DATE:** _____

Emotionally _____

Mentally _____

Physically _____

Spiritually _____

Socially _____

Courage Tools

What can I be thankful for?
Positivity _____

How do I say "stop," "no," "enough"?
Boundaries _____

Who do I need to forgive, including me?
Forgiveness _____

When or how can I confront this issue?
Confidence _____

What are the possibilities or opportunities?
Hope _____

Courage Challenge: What is something you can do or say differently today, which you have perhaps never done or done well before, that will challenge or change your broken pattern?

How do you feel about yourself and your life today?   **DATE:** _____

Emotionally   _____

Mentally   _____

Physically   _____

Spiritually   _____

Socially   _____

Courage Tools

What can I be thankful for?
Positivity _____

How do I say "stop," "no," "enough"?
Boundaries _____

Who do I need to forgive, including me?
Forgiveness _____

When or how can I confront this issue?
Confidence _____

What are the possibilities or opportunities?
Hope _____

Courage Challenge: What is something you can do or say differently today, which you have perhaps never done or done well before, that will challenge or change your broken pattern?

How do you feel about yourself and your life today?   **DATE:** _____

Emotionally   _____

Mentally   _____

Physically   _____

Spiritually   _____

Socially   _____

Courage Tools

What can I be thankful for?
Positivity _____

How do I say "stop," "no," "enough"?
Boundaries _____

Who do I need to forgive, including me?
Forgiveness _____

When or how can I confront this issue?
Confidence _____

What are the possibilities or opportunities?
Hope _____

Courage Challenge: What is something you can do or say differently today, which you have perhaps never done or done well before, that will challenge or change your broken pattern?

How do you feel about yourself and your life today? **DATE:** _____

Emotionally _____

Mentally _____

Physically _____

Spiritually _____

Socially _____

Courage Tools

What can I be thankful for?
Positivity _____

How do I say "stop," "no," "enough"?
Boundaries _____

Who do I need to forgive, including me?
Forgiveness _____

When or how can I confront this issue?
Confidence _____

What are the possibilities or opportunities?
Hope _____

Courage Challenge: What is something you can do or say differently today, which you have perhaps never done or done well before, that will challenge or change your broken pattern?

Weekly
U P D A T E . .

From 1 to 10 with 10 being the best, how did you do this week with confronting, challenging or changing your broken patterns?

_____

Why did you do so well or so poorly?

_____

What is it going to take to get to the next level?

_____

How do you feel about yourself and your life today?   **DATE:** _____

Emotionally _____

Mentally   _____

Physically   _____

Spiritually _____

Socially   _____

Courage Tools

What can I be thankful for?
Positivity _____

How do I say "stop," "no," "enough"?
Boundaries _____

Who do I need to forgive, including me?
Forgiveness _____

When or how can I confront this issue?
Confidence _____

What are the possibilities or opportunities?
Hope _____

Courage Challenge: What is something you can do or say differently today, which you have perhaps never done or done well before, that will challenge or change your broken pattern?

How do you feel about yourself and your life today?   **DATE:** _____

Emotionally _____

Mentally   _____

Physically   _____

Spiritually _____

Socially   _____

Courage Tools

What can I be thankful for?
Positivity _____

How do I say "stop," "no," "enough"?
Boundaries _____

Who do I need to forgive, including me?
Forgiveness _____

When or how can I confront this issue?
Confidence _____

What are the possibilities or opportunities?
Hope _____

Courage Challenge: What is something you can do or say differently today, which you have perhaps never done or done well before, that will challenge or change your broken pattern?

How do you feel about yourself and your life today?   **DATE:** _____

Emotionally   _____
Mentally   _____
Physically   _____
Spiritually   _____
Socially   _____

Courage Tools

What can I be thankful for?
Positivity _____

How do I say "stop," "no," "enough"?
Boundaries _____

Who do I need to forgive, including me?
Forgiveness _____

When or how can I confront this issue?
Confidence _____

What are the possibilities or opportunities?
Hope _____

Courage Challenge: What is something you can do or say differently today, which you have perhaps never done or done well before, that will challenge or change your broken pattern?

DATE: _____

How do you feel about yourself and your life today?

Emotionally _____

Mentally _____

Physically _____

Spiritually _____

Socially _____

Courage Tools

What can I be thankful for?
Positivity _____

How do I say "stop," "no," "enough"?
Boundaries _____

Who do I need to forgive, including me?
Forgiveness _____

When or how can I confront this issue?
Confidence _____

What are the possibilities or opportunities?
Hope _____

Courage Challenge: What is something you can do or say differently today, which you have perhaps never done or done well before, that will challenge or change your broken pattern?

How do you feel about yourself and your life today? **DATE:** _____

Emotionally _____

Mentally _____

Physically _____

Spiritually _____

Socially _____

Courage Tools

What can I be thankful for?
Positivity _____

How do I say "stop," "no," "enough"?
Boundaries _____

Who do I need to forgive, including me?
Forgiveness _____

When or how can I confront this issue?
Confidence _____

What are the possibilities or opportunities?
Hope _____

Courage Challenge: What is something you can do or say differently today, which you have perhaps never done or done well before, that will challenge or change your broken pattern?

How do you feel about yourself and your life today? **DATE:** _____

Emotionally _____

Mentally _____

Physically _____

Spiritually _____

Socially _____

Courage Tools

What can I be thankful for?
Positivity _____

How do I say "stop," "no," "enough"?
Boundaries _____

Who do I need to forgive, including me?
Forgiveness _____

When or how can I confront this issue?
Confidence _____

What are the possibilities or opportunities?
Hope _____

Courage Challenge: What is something you can do or say differently today, which you have perhaps never done or done well before, that will challenge or change your broken pattern?

How do you feel about yourself and your life today?   **DATE:** _____

Emotionally _____

Mentally _____

Physically _____

Spiritually _____

Socially _____

Courage Tools

What can I be thankful for?
Positivity _____

How do I say "stop," "no," "enough"?
Boundaries _____

Who do I need to forgive, including me?
Forgiveness _____

When or how can I confront this issue?
Confidence _____

What are the possibilities or opportunities?
Hope _____

Courage Challenge: What is something you can do or say differently today, which you have perhaps never done or done well before, that will challenge or change your broken pattern?

Weekly
U P D A T E . .

From 1 to 10 with 10 being the best, how did you do this week with confronting, challenging or changing your broken patterns?

_____

Why did you do so well or so poorly?

_____

What is it going to take to get to the next level?

_____

How do you feel about yourself and your life today? **DATE:** _____

Emotionally _____

Mentally _____

Physically _____

Spiritually _____

Socially _____

Courage Tools

What can I be thankful for?
Positivity _____

How do I say "stop," "no," "enough"?
Boundaries _____

Who do I need to forgive, including me?
Forgiveness _____

When or how can I confront this issue?
Confidence _____

What are the possibilities or opportunities?
Hope _____

Courage Challenge: What is something you can do or say differently today, which you have perhaps never done or done well before, that will challenge or change your broken pattern?

How do you feel about yourself and your life today?   **DATE:** _____

Emotionally   _____

Mentally   _____

Physically   _____

Spiritually   _____

Socially   _____

Courage Tools

What can I be thankful for?
Positivity _____

How do I say "stop," "no," "enough"?
Boundaries _____

Who do I need to forgive, including me?
Forgiveness _____

When or how can I confront this issue?
Confidence _____

What are the possibilities or opportunities?
Hope _____

Courage Challenge: What is something you can do or say differently today, which you have perhaps never done or done well before, that will challenge or change your broken pattern?

How do you feel about yourself and your life today?   **DATE:** _____

Emotionally   _____

Mentally   _____

Physically   _____

Spiritually   _____

Socially   _____

Courage Tools

What can I be thankful for?
Positivity _____

How do I say "stop," "no," "enough"?
Boundaries _____

Who do I need to forgive, including me?
Forgiveness _____

When or how can I confront this issue?
Confidence _____

What are the possibilities or opportunities?
Hope _____

Courage Challenge: What is something you can do or say differently today, which you have perhaps never done or done well before, that will challenge or change your broken pattern?

How do you feel about yourself and your life today? **DATE:** _____

Emotionally _____

Mentally _____

Physically _____

Spiritually _____

Socially _____

Courage Tools

What can I be thankful for?
Positivity _____

How do I say "stop," "no," "enough"?
Boundaries _____

Who do I need to forgive, including me?
Forgiveness _____

When or how can I confront this issue?
Confidence _____

What are the possibilities or opportunities?
Hope _____

Courage Challenge: What is something you can do or say differently today, which you have perhaps never done or done well before, that will challenge or change your broken pattern?

How do you feel about yourself and your life today?   **DATE:** _____

Emotionally _____

Mentally   _____

Physically   _____

Spiritually _____

Socially   _____

Courage Tools

What can I be thankful for?
Positivity _____

How do I say "stop," "no," "enough"?
Boundaries _____

Who do I need to forgive, including me?
Forgiveness _____

When or how can I confront this issue?
Confidence _____

What are the possibilities or opportunities?
Hope _____

Courage Challenge: What is something you can do or say differently today, which you have perhaps never done or done well before, that will challenge or change your broken pattern?

How do you feel about yourself and your life today?   **DATE:** _____

Emotionally   _____

Mentally   _____

Physically   _____

Spiritually   _____

Socially   _____

Courage Tools

What can I be thankful for?
Positivity _____

How do I say "stop," "no," "enough"?
Boundaries _____

Who do I need to forgive, including me?
Forgiveness _____

When or how can I confront this issue?
Confidence _____

What are the possibilities or opportunities?
Hope _____

Courage Challenge: What is something you can do or say differently today, which you have perhaps never done or done well before, that will challenge or change your broken pattern?

How do you feel about yourself and your life today?   **DATE:** _____

Emotionally   _____

Mentally   _____

Physically   _____

Spiritually   _____

Socially   _____

Courage Tools

What can I be thankful for?
Positivity _____

How do I say "stop," "no," "enough"?
Boundaries _____

Who do I need to forgive, including me?
Forgiveness _____

When or how can I confront this issue?
Confidence _____

What are the possibilities or opportunities?
Hope _____

Courage Challenge: What is something you can do or say differently today, which you have perhaps never done or done well before, that will challenge or change your broken pattern?

Weekly
U P D A T E . .

From 1 to 10 with 10 being the best, how did you do this week with confronting, challenging or changing your broken patterns?

_____

Why did you do so well or so poorly?

_____

What is it going to take to get to the next level?

_____

> "In the middle of a difficulty lies opportunity."

— ALBERT EINSTEIN —

STRONGER DAYS

Because the first step to restoring your brokenness is admitting that you are broken, think about the aspect of your life that you most need to address this month:

_____

_____

_____

_____

_____

_____

_____

For the next several weeks, think about how you can confront and overcome your issue(s) by writing down your thoughts on the following pages each day.

How do you feel about yourself and your life today?   **DATE:** _____

Emotionally   _____

Mentally   _____

Physically   _____

Spiritually   _____

Socially   _____

Courage Tools

What can I be thankful for?
Positivity _____

How do I say "stop," "no," "enough"?
Boundaries _____

Who do I need to forgive, including me?
Forgiveness _____

When or how can I confront this issue?
Confidence _____

What are the possibilities or opportunities?
Hope _____

Courage Challenge: What is something you can do or say differently today, which you have perhaps never done or done well before, that will challenge or change your broken pattern?

How do you feel about yourself and your life today?   **DATE:** _____

Emotionally   _____

Mentally   _____

Physically   _____

Spiritually   _____

Socially   _____

Courage Tools

What can I be thankful for?
Positivity _____

How do I say "stop," "no," "enough"?
Boundaries _____

Who do I need to forgive, including me?
Forgiveness _____

When or how can I confront this issue?
Confidence _____

What are the possibilities or opportunities?
Hope _____

Courage Challenge: What is something you can do or say differently today, which you have perhaps never done or done well before, that will challenge or change your broken pattern?

How do you feel about yourself and your life today? **DATE:** _____

Emotionally _____

Mentally _____

Physically _____

Spiritually _____

Socially _____

Courage Tools

What can I be thankful for?
Positivity _____

How do I say "stop," "no," "enough"?
Boundaries _____

Who do I need to forgive, including me?
Forgiveness _____

When or how can I confront this issue?
Confidence _____

What are the possibilities or opportunities?
Hope _____

Courage Challenge: What is something you can do or say differently today, which you have perhaps never done or done well before, that will challenge or change your broken pattern?

How do you feel about yourself and your life today?   **DATE:** _____

Emotionally   _____

Mentally   _____

Physically   _____

Spiritually   _____

Socially   _____

Courage Tools

What can I be thankful for?
Positivity _____

How do I say "stop," "no," "enough"?
Boundaries _____

Who do I need to forgive, including me?
Forgiveness _____

When or how can I confront this issue?
Confidence _____

What are the possibilities or opportunities?
Hope _____

Courage Challenge: What is something you can do or say differently today, which you have perhaps never done or done well before, that will challenge or change your broken pattern?

How do you feel about yourself and your life today?   **DATE:** _____

Emotionally   _____

Mentally   _____

Physically   _____

Spiritually   _____

Socially   _____

Courage Tools

What can I be thankful for?
Positivity _____

How do I say "stop," "no," "enough"?
Boundaries _____

Who do I need to forgive, including me?
Forgiveness _____

When or how can I confront this issue?
Confidence _____

What are the possibilities or opportunities?
Hope _____

Courage Challenge: What is something you can do or say differently today, which you have perhaps never done or done well before, that will challenge or change your broken pattern?

How do you feel about yourself and your life today?   **DATE:** _____

Emotionally _____

Mentally _____

Physically _____

Spiritually _____

Socially _____

Courage Tools

What can I be thankful for?
Positivity _____

How do I say "stop," "no," "enough"?
Boundaries _____

Who do I need to forgive, including me?
Forgiveness _____

When or how can I confront this issue?
Confidence _____

What are the possibilities or opportunities?
Hope _____

Courage Challenge: What is something you can do or say differently today, which you have perhaps never done or done well before, that will challenge or change your broken pattern?

How do you feel about yourself and your life today? **DATE:** _____

Emotionally _____

Mentally _____

Physically _____

Spiritually _____

Socially _____

Courage Tools

What can I be thankful for?
Positivity _____

How do I say "stop," "no," "enough"?
Boundaries _____

Who do I need to forgive, including me?
Forgiveness _____

When or how can I confront this issue?
Confidence _____

What are the possibilities or opportunities?
Hope _____

Courage Challenge: What is something you can do or say differently today, which you have perhaps never done or done well before, that will challenge or change your broken pattern?

Weekly
UPDATE..

From 1 to 10 with 10 being the best, how did you do this week with confronting, challenging or changing your broken patterns?

_____

Why did you do so well or so poorly?

_____

What is it going to take to get to the next level?

_____

How do you feel about yourself and your life today? **DATE:** _____

Emotionally _____

Mentally _____

Physically _____

Spiritually _____

Socially _____

Courage Tools

What can I be thankful for?
Positivity _____

How do I say "stop," "no," "enough"?
Boundaries _____

Who do I need to forgive, including me?
Forgiveness _____

When or how can I confront this issue?
Confidence _____

What are the possibilities or opportunities?
Hope _____

Courage Challenge: What is something you can do or say differently today, which you have perhaps never done or done well before, that will challenge or change your broken pattern?

How do you feel about yourself and your life today?   **DATE:** _____

Emotionally   _____

Mentally   _____

Physically   _____

Spiritually   _____

Socially   _____

Courage Tools

What can I be thankful for?
Positivity _____

How do I say "stop," "no," "enough"?
Boundaries _____

Who do I need to forgive, including me?
Forgiveness _____

When or how can I confront this issue?
Confidence _____

What are the possibilities or opportunities?
Hope _____

Courage Challenge: What is something you can do or say differently today, which you have perhaps never done or done well before, that will challenge or change your broken pattern?

How do you feel about yourself and your life today? **DATE:** _____

Emotionally _____

Mentally _____

Physically _____

Spiritually _____

Socially _____

Courage Tools

What can I be thankful for?
Positivity _____

How do I say "stop," "no," "enough"?
Boundaries _____

Who do I need to forgive, including me?
Forgiveness _____

When or how can I confront this issue?
Confidence _____

What are the possibilities or opportunities?
Hope _____

Courage Challenge: What is something you can do or say differently today, which you have perhaps never done or done well before, that will challenge or change your broken pattern?

How do you feel about yourself and your life today?   **DATE:** _____

Emotionally _____

Mentally _____

Physically _____

Spiritually _____

Socially _____

Courage Tools

What can I be thankful for?
Positivity _____

How do I say "stop," "no," "enough"?
Boundaries _____

Who do I need to forgive, including me?
Forgiveness _____

When or how can I confront this issue?
Confidence _____

What are the possibilities or opportunities?
Hope _____

Courage Challenge: What is something you can do or say differently today, which you have perhaps never done or done well before, that will challenge or change your broken pattern?

How do you feel about yourself and your life today?　**DATE:** _____

Emotionally　_____

Mentally　_____

Physically　_____

Spiritually　_____

Socially　_____

Courage Tools

What can I be thankful for?
Positivity _____

How do I say "stop," "no," "enough"?
Boundaries _____

Who do I need to forgive, including me?
Forgiveness _____

When or how can I confront this issue?
Confidence _____

What are the possibilities or opportunities?
Hope _____

Courage Challenge: What is something you can do or say differently today, which you have perhaps never done or done well before, that will challenge or change your broken pattern?

How do you feel about yourself and your life today?   **DATE:** _____

Emotionally   _____

Mentally   _____

Physically   _____

Spiritually   _____

Socially   _____

Courage Tools

What can I be thankful for?
Positivity _____

How do I say "stop," "no," "enough"?
Boundaries _____

Who do I need to forgive, including me?
Forgiveness _____

When or how can I confront this issue?
Confidence _____

What are the possibilities or opportunities?
Hope _____

Courage Challenge: What is something you can do or say differently today, which you have perhaps never done or done well before, that will challenge or change your broken pattern?

How do you feel about yourself and your life today? **DATE:** _____

Emotionally _____

Mentally _____

Physically _____

Spiritually _____

Socially _____

Courage Tools

What can I be thankful for?
Positivity _____

How do I say "stop," "no," "enough"?
Boundaries _____

Who do I need to forgive, including me?
Forgiveness _____

When or how can I confront this issue?
Confidence _____

What are the possibilities or opportunities?
Hope _____

Courage Challenge: What is something you can do or say differently today, which you have perhaps never done or done well before, that will challenge or change your broken pattern?

Weekly
U P D A T E . .

From 1 to 10 with 10 being the best, how did you do this week with confronting, challenging or changing your broken patterns?

_____

Why did you do so well or so poorly?

_____

What is it going to take to get to the next level?

_____

How do you feel about yourself and your life today? **DATE:** _____

Emotionally _____

Mentally _____

Physically _____

Spiritually _____

Socially _____

Courage Tools

What can I be thankful for?
Positivity _____

How do I say "stop," "no," "enough"?
Boundaries _____

Who do I need to forgive, including me?
Forgiveness _____

When or how can I confront this issue?
Confidence _____

What are the possibilities or opportunities?
Hope _____

Courage Challenge: What is something you can do or say differently today, which you have perhaps never done or done well before, that will challenge or change your broken pattern?

How do you feel about yourself and your life today? **DATE:** _____

Emotionally _____

Mentally _____

Physically _____

Spiritually _____

Socially _____

Courage Tools

What can I be thankful for?
Positivity _____

How do I say "stop," "no," "enough"?
Boundaries _____

Who do I need to forgive, including me?
Forgiveness _____

When or how can I confront this issue?
Confidence _____

What are the possibilities or opportunities?
Hope _____

Courage Challenge: What is something you can do or say differently today, which you have perhaps never done or done well before, that will challenge or change your broken pattern?

How do you feel about yourself and your life today? **DATE:** _____

Emotionally _____

Mentally   _____

Physically   _____

Spiritually _____

Socially   _____

Courage Tools

What can I be thankful for?
Positivity _____

How do I say "stop," "no," "enough"?
Boundaries _____

Who do I need to forgive, including me?
Forgiveness _____

When or how can I confront this issue?
Confidence _____

What are the possibilities or opportunities?
Hope _____

Courage Challenge: What is something you can do or say differently today, which you have perhaps never done or done well before, that will challenge or change your broken pattern?

How do you feel about yourself and your life today? **DATE:** _____

Emotionally _____

Mentally _____

Physically _____

Spiritually _____

Socially _____

Courage Tools

What can I be thankful for?
Positivity _____

How do I say "stop," "no," "enough"?
Boundaries _____

Who do I need to forgive, including me?
Forgiveness _____

When or how can I confront this issue?
Confidence _____

What are the possibilities or opportunities?
Hope _____

Courage Challenge: What is something you can do or say differently today, which you have perhaps never done or done well before, that will challenge or change your broken pattern?

How do you feel about yourself and your life today?   **DATE:** _____

Emotionally   _____

Mentally   _____

Physically   _____

Spiritually   _____

Socially   _____

Courage Tools

What can I be thankful for?
Positivity _____

How do I say "stop," "no," "enough"?
Boundaries _____

Who do I need to forgive, including me?
Forgiveness _____

When or how can I confront this issue?
Confidence _____

What are the possibilities or opportunities?
Hope _____

Courage Challenge: What is something you can do or say differently today, which you have perhaps never done or done well before, that will challenge or change your broken pattern?

How do you feel about yourself and your life today?   **DATE:** _____

Emotionally   _____

Mentally   _____

Physically   _____

Spiritually   _____

Socially   _____

Courage Tools

What can I be thankful for?
Positivity _____

How do I say "stop," "no," "enough"?
Boundaries _____

Who do I need to forgive, including me?
Forgiveness _____

When or how can I confront this issue?
Confidence _____

What are the possibilities or opportunities?
Hope _____

Courage Challenge: What is something you can do or say differently today, which you have perhaps never done or done well before, that will challenge or change your broken pattern?

How do you feel about yourself and your life today?   **DATE:** _____

Emotionally _____

Mentally   _____

Physically   _____

Spiritually _____

Socially   _____

Courage Tools

What can I be thankful for?
Positivity _____

How do I say "stop," "no," "enough"?
Boundaries _____

Who do I need to forgive, including me?
Forgiveness _____

When or how can I confront this issue?
Confidence _____

What are the possibilities or opportunities?
Hope _____

Courage Challenge: What is something you can do or say differently today, which you have perhaps never done or done well before, that will challenge or change your broken pattern?

U P D A T E . .

From 1 to 10 with 10 being the best, how did you do this week with confronting, challenging or changing your broken patterns?

_____

Why did you do so well or so poorly?

_____

What is it going to take to get to the next level?

_____

How do you feel about yourself and your life today?   **DATE:** _____

Emotionally   _____

Mentally   _____

Physically   _____

Spiritually   _____

Socially   _____

Courage Tools

What can I be thankful for?
Positivity _____

How do I say "stop," "no," "enough"?
Boundaries _____

Who do I need to forgive, including me?
Forgiveness _____

When or how can I confront this issue?
Confidence _____

What are the possibilities or opportunities?
Hope _____

Courage Challenge: What is something you can do or say differently today, which you have perhaps never done or done well before, that will challenge or change your broken pattern?

How do you feel about yourself and your life today? **DATE:** _____

Emotionally _____

Mentally _____

Physically _____

Spiritually _____

Socially _____

Courage Tools

What can I be thankful for?
Positivity _____

How do I say "stop," "no," "enough"?
Boundaries _____

Who do I need to forgive, including me?
Forgiveness _____

When or how can I confront this issue?
Confidence _____

What are the possibilities or opportunities?
Hope _____

Courage Challenge: What is something you can do or say differently today, which you have perhaps never done or done well before, that will challenge or change your broken pattern?

How do you feel about yourself and your life today? **DATE:** _____

Emotionally _____

Mentally _____

Physically _____

Spiritually _____

Socially _____

Courage Tools

What can I be thankful for?
Positivity _____

How do I say "stop," "no," "enough"?
Boundaries _____

Who do I need to forgive, including me?
Forgiveness _____

When or how can I confront this issue?
Confidence _____

What are the possibilities or opportunities?
Hope _____

Courage Challenge: What is something you can do or say differently today, which you have perhaps never done or done well before, that will challenge or change your broken pattern?

How do you feel about yourself and your life today? **DATE:** _____

Emotionally _____

Mentally _____

Physically _____

Spiritually _____

Socially _____

Courage Tools

What can I be thankful for?
Positivity _____

How do I say "stop," "no," "enough"?
Boundaries _____

Who do I need to forgive, including me?
Forgiveness _____

When or how can I confront this issue?
Confidence _____

What are the possibilities or opportunities?
Hope _____

Courage Challenge: What is something you can do or say differently today, which you have perhaps never done or done well before, that will challenge or change your broken pattern?

How do you feel about yourself and your life today? **DATE:** _____

Emotionally _____

Mentally _____

Physically _____

Spiritually _____

Socially _____

Courage Tools

What can I be thankful for?
Positivity _____

How do I say "stop," "no," "enough"?
Boundaries _____

Who do I need to forgive, including me?
Forgiveness _____

When or how can I confront this issue?
Confidence _____

What are the possibilities or opportunities?
Hope _____

Courage Challenge: What is something you can do or say differently today, which you have perhaps never done or done well before, that will challenge or change your broken pattern?

How do you feel about yourself and your life today?   **DATE:** _____

Emotionally   _____

Mentally   _____

Physically   _____

Spiritually   _____

Socially   _____

Courage Tools

What can I be thankful for?
Positivity _____

How do I say "stop," "no," "enough"?
Boundaries _____

Who do I need to forgive, including me?
Forgiveness _____

When or how can I confront this issue?
Confidence _____

What are the possibilities or opportunities?
Hope _____

Courage Challenge: What is something you can do or say differently today, which you have perhaps never done or done well before, that will challenge or change your broken pattern?

How do you feel about yourself and your life today?   **DATE:** _____

Emotionally _____

Mentally _____

Physically _____

Spiritually _____

Socially _____

Courage Tools

What can I be thankful for?
Positivity _____

How do I say "stop," "no," "enough"?
Boundaries _____

Who do I need to forgive, including me?
Forgiveness _____

When or how can I confront this issue?
Confidence _____

What are the possibilities or opportunities?
Hope _____

Courage Challenge: What is something you can do or say differently today, which you have perhaps never done or done well before, that will challenge or change your broken pattern?

Weekly
U P D A T E . .

From 1 to 10 with 10 being the best, how did you do this week with confronting, challenging or changing your broken patterns?

_____

Why did you do so well or so poorly?

_____

What is it going to take to get to the next level?

_____

> "So do not fear, for I am with you; do not be dismayed, for I am your God. I will strengthen you and help you; I will uphold you with my righteous right hand."

— ISAIAH 41:10 —

STRONGER DAYS

Because the first step to restoring your brokenness is admitting that you are broken, think about the aspect of your life that you most need to address this month:

_____

_____

_____

_____

_____

_____

_____

For the next several weeks, think about how you can confront and overcome your issue(s) by writing down your thoughts on the following pages each day.

How do you feel about yourself and your life today?   **DATE:** _____

Emotionally _____

Mentally   _____

Physically   _____

Spiritually _____

Socially   _____

Courage Tools

What can I be thankful for?
Positivity _____

How do I say "stop," "no," "enough"?
Boundaries _____

Who do I need to forgive, including me?
Forgiveness _____

When or how can I confront this issue?
Confidence _____

What are the possibilities or opportunities?
Hope _____

Courage Challenge: What is something you can do or say differently today, which you have perhaps never done or done well before, that will challenge or change your broken pattern?

How do you feel about yourself and your life today? **DATE:** _____

Emotionally _____

Mentally _____

Physically _____

Spiritually _____

Socially _____

Courage Tools

What can I be thankful for?
Positivity _____

How do I say "stop," "no," "enough"?
Boundaries _____

Who do I need to forgive, including me?
Forgiveness _____

When or how can I confront this issue?
Confidence _____

What are the possibilities or opportunities?
Hope _____

Courage Challenge: What is something you can do or say differently today, which you have perhaps never done or done well before, that will challenge or change your broken pattern?

How do you feel about yourself and your life today? **DATE:** _____

Emotionally _____

Mentally _____

Physically _____

Spiritually _____

Socially _____

Courage Tools

What can I be thankful for?
Positivity _____

How do I say "stop," "no," "enough"?
Boundaries _____

Who do I need to forgive, including me?
Forgiveness _____

When or how can I confront this issue?
Confidence _____

What are the possibilities or opportunities?
Hope _____

Courage Challenge: What is something you can do or say differently today, which you have perhaps never done or done well before, that will challenge or change your broken pattern?

How do you feel about yourself and your life today? **DATE:** _____

Emotionally _____
Mentally _____
Physically _____
Spiritually _____
Socially _____

Courage Tools

What can I be thankful for?
Positivity _____

How do I say "stop," "no," "enough"?
Boundaries _____

Who do I need to forgive, including me?
Forgiveness _____

When or how can I confront this issue?
Confidence _____

What are the possibilities or opportunities?
Hope _____

Courage Challenge: What is something you can do or say differently today, which you have perhaps never done or done well before, that will challenge or change your broken pattern?

How do you feel about yourself and your life today?   **DATE:** _____

Emotionally   _____

Mentally   _____

Physically   _____

Spiritually   _____

Socially   _____

Courage Tools

What can I be thankful for?
Positivity _____

How do I say "stop," "no," "enough"?
Boundaries _____

Who do I need to forgive, including me?
Forgiveness _____

When or how can I confront this issue?
Confidence _____

What are the possibilities or opportunities?
Hope _____

Courage Challenge: What is something you can do or say differently today, which you have perhaps never done or done well before, that will challenge or change your broken pattern?

How do you feel about yourself and your life today?   **DATE:** _____

Emotionally   _____

Mentally   _____

Physically   _____

Spiritually   _____

Socially   _____

Courage Tools

What can I be thankful for?
Positivity _____

How do I say "stop," "no," "enough"?
Boundaries _____

Who do I need to forgive, including me?
Forgiveness _____

When or how can I confront this issue?
Confidence _____

What are the possibilities or opportunities?
Hope _____

Courage Challenge: What is something you can do or say differently today, which you have perhaps never done or done well before, that will challenge or change your broken pattern?

How do you feel about yourself and your life today?   **DATE:** _____

Emotionally _____

Mentally _____

Physically _____

Spiritually _____

Socially _____

Courage Tools

What can I be thankful for?
Positivity _____

How do I say "stop," "no," "enough"?
Boundaries _____

Who do I need to forgive, including me?
Forgiveness _____

When or how can I confront this issue?
Confidence _____

What are the possibilities or opportunities?
Hope _____

Courage Challenge: What is something you can do or say differently today, which you have perhaps never done or done well before, that will challenge or change your broken pattern?

From 1 to 10 with 10 being the best, how did you do this week with confronting, challenging or changing your broken patterns?

_____

Why did you do so well or so poorly?

_____

What is it going to take to get to the next level?

_____

How do you feel about yourself and your life today? **DATE:** _____

Emotionally _____

Mentally _____

Physically _____

Spiritually _____

Socially _____

Courage Tools

What can I be thankful for?
Positivity _____

How do I say "stop," "no," "enough"?
Boundaries _____

Who do I need to forgive, including me?
Forgiveness _____

When or how can I confront this issue?
Confidence _____

What are the possibilities or opportunities?
Hope _____

Courage Challenge: What is something you can do or say differently today, which you have perhaps never done or done well before, that will challenge or change your broken pattern?

How do you feel about yourself and your life today? **DATE:** _____

Emotionally _____

Mentally _____

Physically _____

Spiritually _____

Socially _____

Courage Tools

What can I be thankful for?
Positivity _____

How do I say "stop," "no," "enough"?
Boundaries _____

Who do I need to forgive, including me?
Forgiveness _____

When or how can I confront this issue?
Confidence _____

What are the possibilities or opportunities?
Hope _____

Courage Challenge: What is something you can do or say differently today, which you have perhaps never done or done well before, that will challenge or change your broken pattern?

How do you feel about yourself and your life today? **DATE:** _____

Emotionally _____

Mentally _____

Physically _____

Spiritually _____

Socially _____

Courage Tools

What can I be thankful for?
Positivity _____

How do I say "stop," "no," "enough"?
Boundaries _____

Who do I need to forgive, including me?
Forgiveness _____

When or how can I confront this issue?
Confidence _____

What are the possibilities or opportunities?
Hope _____

Courage Challenge: What is something you can do or say differently today, which you have perhaps never done or done well before, that will challenge or change your broken pattern?

How do you feel about yourself and your life today? **DATE:** _____

Emotionally _____

Mentally _____

Physically _____

Spiritually _____

Socially _____

Courage Tools

What can I be thankful for?
Positivity _____

How do I say "stop," "no," "enough"?
Boundaries _____

Who do I need to forgive, including me?
Forgiveness _____

When or how can I confront this issue?
Confidence _____

What are the possibilities or opportunities?
Hope _____

Courage Challenge: What is something you can do or say differently today, which you have perhaps never done or done well before, that will challenge or change your broken pattern?

How do you feel about yourself and your life today? **DATE:** _____

Emotionally _____

Mentally   _____

Physically   _____

Spiritually _____

Socially   _____

Courage Tools

What can I be thankful for?
Positivity _____

How do I say "stop," "no," "enough"?
Boundaries _____

Who do I need to forgive, including me?
Forgiveness _____

When or how can I confront this issue?
Confidence _____

What are the possibilities or opportunities?
Hope _____

Courage Challenge: What is something you can do or say differently today, which you have perhaps never done or done well before, that will challenge or change your broken pattern?

How do you feel about yourself and your life today?   **DATE:** _____

Emotionally   _____

Mentally   _____

Physically   _____

Spiritually   _____

Socially   _____

Courage Tools

What can I be thankful for?
Positivity _____

How do I say "stop," "no," "enough"?
Boundaries _____

Who do I need to forgive, including me?
Forgiveness _____

When or how can I confront this issue?
Confidence _____

What are the possibilities or opportunities?
Hope _____

Courage Challenge: What is something you can do or say differently today, which you have perhaps never done or done well before, that will challenge or change your broken pattern?

How do you feel about yourself and your life today?   **DATE:** _____

Emotionally   _____

Mentally   _____

Physically   _____

Spiritually   _____

Socially   _____

Courage Tools

What can I be thankful for?
Positivity _____

How do I say "stop," "no," "enough"?
Boundaries _____

Who do I need to forgive, including me?
Forgiveness _____

When or how can I confront this issue?
Confidence _____

What are the possibilities or opportunities?
Hope _____

Courage Challenge: What is something you can do or say differently today, which you have perhaps never done or done well before, that will challenge or change your broken pattern?

From 1 to 10 with 10 being the best, how did you do this week with confronting, challenging or changing your broken patterns?

_____

Why did you do so well or so poorly?

_____

What is it going to take to get to the next level?

_____

How do you feel about yourself and your life today? **DATE:** _____

Emotionally _____

Mentally _____

Physically _____

Spiritually _____

Socially _____

Courage Tools

What can I be thankful for?
Positivity _____

How do I say "stop," "no," "enough"?
Boundaries _____

Who do I need to forgive, including me?
Forgiveness _____

When or how can I confront this issue?
Confidence _____

What are the possibilities or opportunities?
Hope _____

Courage Challenge: What is something you can do or say differently today, which you have perhaps never done or done well before, that will challenge or change your broken pattern?

How do you feel about yourself and your life today? **DATE:** _____

Emotionally _____

Mentally _____

Physically _____

Spiritually _____

Socially _____

Courage Tools

What can I be thankful for?
Positivity _____

How do I say "stop," "no," "enough"?
Boundaries _____

Who do I need to forgive, including me?
Forgiveness _____

When or how can I confront this issue?
Confidence _____

What are the possibilities or opportunities?
Hope _____

Courage Challenge: What is something you can do or say differently today, which you have perhaps never done or done well before, that will challenge or change your broken pattern?

How do you feel about yourself and your life today? **DATE:** _____

Emotionally _____

Mentally _____

Physically _____

Spiritually _____

Socially _____

Courage Tools

What can I be thankful for?
Positivity _____

How do I say "stop," "no," "enough"?
Boundaries _____

Who do I need to forgive, including me?
Forgiveness _____

When or how can I confront this issue?
Confidence _____

What are the possibilities or opportunities?
Hope _____

Courage Challenge: What is something you can do or say differently today, which you have perhaps never done or done well before, that will challenge or change your broken pattern?

How do you feel about yourself and your life today? **DATE:** _____

Emotionally _____
Mentally _____
Physically _____
Spiritually _____
Socially _____

Courage Tools

What can I be thankful for?
Positivity _____

How do I say "stop," "no," "enough"?
Boundaries _____

Who do I need to forgive, including me?
Forgiveness _____

When or how can I confront this issue?
Confidence _____

What are the possibilities or opportunities?
Hope _____

Courage Challenge: What is something you can do or say differently today, which you have perhaps never done or done well before, that will challenge or change your broken pattern?

How do you feel about yourself and your life today? **DATE:** _____

Emotionally _____

Mentally _____

Physically _____

Spiritually _____

Socially _____

Courage Tools

What can I be thankful for?
Positivity _____

How do I say "stop," "no," "enough"?
Boundaries _____

Who do I need to forgive, including me?
Forgiveness _____

When or how can I confront this issue?
Confidence _____

What are the possibilities or opportunities?
Hope _____

Courage Challenge: What is something you can do or say differently today, which you have perhaps never done or done well before, that will challenge or change your broken pattern?

How do you feel about yourself and your life today? **DATE:** _____

Emotionally _____

Mentally _____

Physically _____

Spiritually _____

Socially _____

Courage Tools

What can I be thankful for?
Positivity _____

How do I say "stop," "no," "enough"?
Boundaries _____

Who do I need to forgive, including me?
Forgiveness _____

When or how can I confront this issue?
Confidence _____

What are the possibilities or opportunities?
Hope _____

Courage Challenge: What is something you can do or say differently today, which you have perhaps never done or done well before, that will challenge or change your broken pattern?

How do you feel about yourself and your life today?   **DATE:** _____

Emotionally   _____

Mentally   _____

Physically   _____

Spiritually   _____

Socially   _____

Courage Tools

What can I be thankful for?
Positivity _____

How do I say "stop," "no," "enough"?
Boundaries _____

Who do I need to forgive, including me?
Forgiveness _____

When or how can I confront this issue?
Confidence _____

What are the possibilities or opportunities?
Hope _____

Courage Challenge: What is something you can do or say differently today, which you have perhaps never done or done well before, that will challenge or change your broken pattern?

Weekly
U P D A T E . .

From 1 to 10 with 10 being the best, how did you do this week with confronting, challenging or changing your broken patterns?

_____

Why did you do so well or so poorly?

_____

What is it going to take to get to the next level?

_____

How do you feel about yourself and your life today? **DATE:** _____

Emotionally _____

Mentally _____

Physically _____

Spiritually _____

Socially _____

Courage Tools

What can I be thankful for?
Positivity _____

How do I say "stop," "no," "enough"?
Boundaries _____

Who do I need to forgive, including me?
Forgiveness _____

When or how can I confront this issue?
Confidence _____

What are the possibilities or opportunities?
Hope _____

Courage Challenge: What is something you can do or say differently today, which you have perhaps never done or done well before, that will challenge or change your broken pattern?

How do you feel about yourself and your life today? **DATE:** _____

Emotionally _____

Mentally _____

Physically _____

Spiritually _____

Socially _____

Courage Tools

What can I be thankful for?
Positivity _____

How do I say "stop," "no," "enough"?
Boundaries _____

Who do I need to forgive, including me?
Forgiveness _____

When or how can I confront this issue?
Confidence _____

What are the possibilities or opportunities?
Hope _____

Courage Challenge: What is something you can do or say differently today, which you have perhaps never done or done well before, that will challenge or change your broken pattern?

How do you feel about yourself and your life today?   **DATE:** _____

Emotionally _____

Mentally _____

Physically _____

Spiritually _____

Socially _____

Courage Tools

What can I be thankful for?
Positivity _____

How do I say "stop," "no," "enough"?
Boundaries _____

Who do I need to forgive, including me?
Forgiveness _____

When or how can I confront this issue?
Confidence _____

What are the possibilities or opportunities?
Hope _____

Courage Challenge: What is something you can do or say differently today, which you have perhaps never done or done well before, that will challenge or change your broken pattern?

How do you feel about yourself and your life today?   **DATE:** _____

Emotionally _____

Mentally   _____

Physically   _____

Spiritually _____

Socially   _____

Courage Tools

What can I be thankful for?
Positivity _____

How do I say "stop," "no," "enough"?
Boundaries _____

Who do I need to forgive, including me?
Forgiveness _____

When or how can I confront this issue?
Confidence _____

What are the possibilities or opportunities?
Hope _____

Courage Challenge: What is something you can do or say differently today, which you have perhaps never done or done well before, that will challenge or change your broken pattern?

How do you feel about yourself and your life today?   **DATE:** _____

Emotionally _____

Mentally _____

Physically _____

Spiritually _____

Socially _____

Courage Tools

What can I be thankful for?
Positivity _____

How do I say "stop," "no," "enough"?
Boundaries _____

Who do I need to forgive, including me?
Forgiveness _____

When or how can I confront this issue?
Confidence _____

What are the possibilities or opportunities?
Hope _____

Courage Challenge: What is something you can do or say differently today, which you have perhaps never done or done well before, that will challenge or change your broken pattern?

How do you feel about yourself and your life today?   **DATE:** _____

Emotionally   _____

Mentally   _____

Physically   _____

Spiritually   _____

Socially   _____

Courage Tools

What can I be thankful for?
Positivity _____

How do I say "stop," "no," "enough"?
Boundaries _____

Who do I need to forgive, including me?
Forgiveness _____

When or how can I confront this issue?
Confidence _____

What are the possibilities or opportunities?
Hope _____

Courage Challenge: What is something you can do or say differently today, which you have perhaps never done or done well before, that will challenge or change your broken pattern?

How do you feel about yourself and your life today? **DATE:** _____

Emotionally _____

Mentally _____

Physically _____

Spiritually _____

Socially _____

Courage Tools

What can I be thankful for?
Positivity _____

How do I say "stop," "no," "enough"?
Boundaries _____

Who do I need to forgive, including me?
Forgiveness _____

When or how can I confront this issue?
Confidence _____

What are the possibilities or opportunities?
Hope _____

Courage Challenge: What is something you can do or say differently today, which you have perhaps never done or done well before, that will challenge or change your broken pattern?

Weekly
U P D A T E . .

From 1 to 10 with 10 being the best, how did you do this week with confronting, challenging or changing your broken patterns?

_____

Why did you do so well or so poorly?

_____

What is it going to take to get to the next level?

_____

> "Strength does not come from physical capacity. It comes from an indomitable will."

— MAHATMA GANDHI —

STRONGER DAYS

Because the first step to restoring your brokenness is admitting that you are broken, think about the aspect of your life that you most need to address this month:

_____

_____

_____

_____

_____

_____

_____

For the next several weeks, think about how you can confront and overcome your issue(s) by writing down your thoughts on the following pages each day.

How do you feel about yourself and your life today?   **DATE:** _____

Emotionally   _____

Mentally   _____

Physically   _____

Spiritually   _____

Socially   _____

Courage Tools

What can I be thankful for?
Positivity _____

How do I say "stop," "no," "enough"?
Boundaries _____

Who do I need to forgive, including me?
Forgiveness _____

When or how can I confront this issue?
Confidence _____

What are the possibilities or opportunities?
Hope _____

Courage Challenge: What is something you can do or say differently today, which you have perhaps never done or done well before, that will challenge or change your broken pattern?

How do you feel about yourself and your life today? **DATE:** _____

Emotionally _____

Mentally _____

Physically _____

Spiritually _____

Socially _____

Courage Tools

What can I be thankful for?
Positivity _____

How do I say "stop," "no," "enough"?
Boundaries _____

Who do I need to forgive, including me?
Forgiveness _____

When or how can I confront this issue?
Confidence _____

What are the possibilities or opportunities?
Hope _____

Courage Challenge: What is something you can do or say differently today, which you have perhaps never done or done well before, that will challenge or change your broken pattern?

How do you feel about yourself and your life today? **DATE:** _____

Emotionally _____

Mentally _____

Physically _____

Spiritually _____

Socially _____

Courage Tools

What can I be thankful for?
Positivity _____

How do I say "stop," "no," "enough"?
Boundaries _____

Who do I need to forgive, including me?
Forgiveness _____

When or how can I confront this issue?
Confidence _____

What are the possibilities or opportunities?
Hope _____

Courage Challenge: What is something you can do or say differently today, which you have perhaps never done or done well before, that will challenge or change your broken pattern?

How do you feel about yourself and your life today? **DATE:** _____

Emotionally _____

Mentally _____

Physically _____

Spiritually _____

Socially _____

Courage Tools

What can I be thankful for?
Positivity _____

How do I say "stop," "no," "enough"?
Boundaries _____

Who do I need to forgive, including me?
Forgiveness _____

When or how can I confront this issue?
Confidence _____

What are the possibilities or opportunities?
Hope _____

Courage Challenge: What is something you can do or say differently today, which you have perhaps never done or done well before, that will challenge or change your broken pattern?

How do you feel about yourself and your life today? **DATE:** _____

Emotionally _____

Mentally _____

Physically _____

Spiritually _____

Socially _____

Courage Tools

What can I be thankful for?
Positivity _____

How do I say "stop," "no," "enough"?
Boundaries _____

Who do I need to forgive, including me?
Forgiveness _____

When or how can I confront this issue?
Confidence _____

What are the possibilities or opportunities?
Hope _____

Courage Challenge: What is something you can do or say differently today, which you have perhaps never done or done well before, that will challenge or change your broken pattern?

How do you feel about yourself and your life today?   **DATE:** _____

Emotionally _____

Mentally _____

Physically _____

Spiritually _____

Socially _____

Courage Tools

What can I be thankful for?
Positivity _____

How do I say "stop," "no," "enough"?
Boundaries _____

Who do I need to forgive, including me?
Forgiveness _____

When or how can I confront this issue?
Confidence _____

What are the possibilities or opportunities?
Hope _____

Courage Challenge: What is something you can do or say differently today, which you have perhaps never done or done well before, that will challenge or change your broken pattern?

How do you feel about yourself and your life today? **DATE:** _____

Emotionally _____

Mentally _____

Physically _____

Spiritually _____

Socially _____

Courage Tools

What can I be thankful for?
Positivity _____

How do I say "stop," "no," "enough"?
Boundaries _____

Who do I need to forgive, including me?
Forgiveness _____

When or how can I confront this issue?
Confidence _____

What are the possibilities or opportunities?
Hope _____

Courage Challenge: What is something you can do or say differently today, which you have perhaps never done or done well before, that will challenge or change your broken pattern?

From 1 to 10 with 10 being the best, how did you do this week with confronting, challenging or changing your broken patterns?

_____

Why did you do so well or so poorly?

_____

What is it going to take to get to the next level?

_____

How do you feel about yourself and your life today?   **DATE:** _____

Emotionally _____

Mentally   _____

Physically   _____

Spiritually _____

Socially   _____

Courage Tools

What can I be thankful for?
Positivity _____

How do I say "stop," "no," "enough"?
Boundaries _____

Who do I need to forgive, including me?
Forgiveness _____

When or how can I confront this issue?
Confidence _____

What are the possibilities or opportunities?
Hope _____

Courage Challenge: What is something you can do or say differently today, which you have perhaps never done or done well before, that will challenge or change your broken pattern?

How do you feel about yourself and your life today? **DATE:** _____

Emotionally   _____
Mentally   _____
Physically   _____
Spiritually   _____
Socially   _____

Courage Tools

What can I be thankful for?
Positivity _____

How do I say "stop," "no," "enough"?
Boundaries _____

Who do I need to forgive, including me?
Forgiveness _____

When or how can I confront this issue?
Confidence _____

What are the possibilities or opportunities?
Hope _____

Courage Challenge: What is something you can do or say differently today, which you have perhaps never done or done well before, that will challenge or change your broken pattern?

How do you feel about yourself and your life today? **DATE:** _____

Emotionally _____

Mentally _____

Physically _____

Spiritually _____

Socially _____

Courage Tools

What can I be thankful for?
Positivity _____

How do I say "stop," "no," "enough"?
Boundaries _____

Who do I need to forgive, including me?
Forgiveness _____

When or how can I confront this issue?
Confidence _____

What are the possibilities or opportunities?
Hope _____

Courage Challenge: What is something you can do or say differently today, which you have perhaps never done or done well before, that will challenge or change your broken pattern?

How do you feel about yourself and your life today? **DATE:** _____

Emotionally _____

Mentally _____

Physically _____

Spiritually _____

Socially _____

Courage Tools

What can I be thankful for?
Positivity _____

How do I say "stop," "no," "enough"?
Boundaries _____

Who do I need to forgive, including me?
Forgiveness _____

When or how can I confront this issue?
Confidence _____

What are the possibilities or opportunities?
Hope _____

Courage Challenge: What is something you can do or say differently today, which you have perhaps never done or done well before, that will challenge or change your broken pattern?

How do you feel about yourself and your life today?   **DATE:** _____

Emotionally   _____

Mentally   _____

Physically   _____

Spiritually   _____

Socially   _____

Courage Tools

What can I be thankful for?
Positivity _____

How do I say "stop," "no," "enough"?
Boundaries _____

Who do I need to forgive, including me?
Forgiveness _____

When or how can I confront this issue?
Confidence _____

What are the possibilities or opportunities?
Hope _____

Courage Challenge: What is something you can do or say differently today, which you have perhaps never done or done well before, that will challenge or change your broken pattern?

How do you feel about yourself and your life today?   **DATE:** _____

Emotionally _____

Mentally _____

Physically _____

Spiritually _____

Socially _____

Courage Tools

What can I be thankful for?
Positivity _____

How do I say "stop," "no," "enough"?
Boundaries _____

Who do I need to forgive, including me?
Forgiveness _____

When or how can I confront this issue?
Confidence _____

What are the possibilities or opportunities?
Hope _____

Courage Challenge: What is something you can do or say differently today, which you have perhaps never done or done well before, that will challenge or change your broken pattern?

How do you feel about yourself and your life today?   **DATE:**

Emotionally _____

Mentally _____

Physically _____

Spiritually _____

Socially _____

Courage Tools

What can I be thankful for?
Positivity _____

How do I say "stop," "no," "enough"?
Boundaries _____

Who do I need to forgive, including me?
Forgiveness _____

When or how can I confront this issue?
Confidence _____

What are the possibilities or opportunities?
Hope _____

Courage Challenge: What is something you can do or say differently today, which you have perhaps never done or done well before, that will challenge or change your broken pattern?

Weekly
U P D A T E . .

From 1 to 10 with 10 being the best, how did you do this week with confronting, challenging or changing your broken patterns?

_____

Why did you do so well or so poorly?

_____

What is it going to take to get to the next level?

_____

How do you feel about yourself and your life today? **DATE:** _____

Emotionally _____

Mentally _____

Physically _____

Spiritually _____

Socially _____

Courage Tools

What can I be thankful for?
Positivity _____

How do I say "stop," "no," "enough"?
Boundaries _____

Who do I need to forgive, including me?
Forgiveness _____

When or how can I confront this issue?
Confidence _____

What are the possibilities or opportunities?
Hope _____

Courage Challenge: What is something you can do or say differently today, which you have perhaps never done or done well before, that will challenge or change your broken pattern?

How do you feel about yourself and your life today?   **DATE:** _____

Emotionally   _____

Mentally   _____

Physically   _____

Spiritually   _____

Socially   _____

Courage Tools

What can I be thankful for?
Positivity _____

How do I say "stop," "no," "enough"?
Boundaries _____

Who do I need to forgive, including me?
Forgiveness _____

When or how can I confront this issue?
Confidence _____

What are the possibilities or opportunities?
Hope _____

Courage Challenge: What is something you can do or say differently today, which you have perhaps never done or done well before, that will challenge or change your broken pattern?

How do you feel about yourself and your life today?   **DATE:** _____

Emotionally   _____

Mentally   _____

Physically   _____

Spiritually   _____

Socially   _____

Courage Tools

What can I be thankful for?
Positivity _____

How do I say "stop," "no," "enough"?
Boundaries _____

Who do I need to forgive, including me?
Forgiveness _____

When or how can I confront this issue?
Confidence _____

What are the possibilities or opportunities?
Hope _____

Courage Challenge: What is something you can do or say differently today, which you have perhaps never done or done well before, that will challenge or change your broken pattern?

DATE: _____

How do you feel about yourself and your life today?

Emotionally   _____

Mentally   _____

Physically   _____

Spiritually   _____

Socially   _____

Courage Tools

What can I be thankful for?
Positivity _____

How do I say "stop," "no," "enough"?
Boundaries _____

Who do I need to forgive, including me?
Forgiveness _____

When or how can I confront this issue?
Confidence _____

What are the possibilities or opportunities?
Hope _____

Courage Challenge: What is something you can do or say differently today, which you have perhaps never done or done well before, that will challenge or change your broken pattern?

How do you feel about yourself and your life today?   **DATE:** _____

Emotionally   _____

Mentally   _____

Physically   _____

Spiritually   _____

Socially   _____

Courage Tools

What can I be thankful for?
Positivity _____

How do I say "stop," "no," "enough"?
Boundaries _____

Who do I need to forgive, including me?
Forgiveness _____

When or how can I confront this issue?
Confidence _____

What are the possibilities or opportunities?
Hope _____

Courage Challenge: What is something you can do or say differently today, which you have perhaps never done or done well before, that will challenge or change your broken pattern?

How do you feel about yourself and your life today? **DATE:** _____

Emotionally _____

Mentally _____

Physically _____

Spiritually _____

Socially _____

Courage Tools

What can I be thankful for?
Positivity _____

How do I say "stop," "no," "enough"?
Boundaries _____

Who do I need to forgive, including me?
Forgiveness _____

When or how can I confront this issue?
Confidence _____

What are the possibilities or opportunities?
Hope _____

Courage Challenge: What is something you can do or say differently today, which you have perhaps never done or done well before, that will challenge or change your broken pattern?

How do you feel about yourself and your life today? **DATE:** _____

Emotionally _____

Mentally _____

Physically _____

Spiritually _____

Socially _____

Courage Tools

What can I be thankful for?
Positivity _____

How do I say "stop," "no," "enough"?
Boundaries _____

Who do I need to forgive, including me?
Forgiveness _____

When or how can I confront this issue?
Confidence _____

What are the possibilities or opportunities?
Hope _____

Courage Challenge: What is something you can do or say differently today, which you have perhaps never done or done well before, that will challenge or change your broken pattern?

Weekly
U P D A T E . .

From 1 to 10 with 10 being the best, how did you do this week with confronting, challenging or changing your broken patterns?

_____

Why did you do so well or so poorly?

_____

What is it going to take to get to the next level?

_____

How do you feel about yourself and your life today? **DATE:** _____

Emotionally _____

Mentally _____

Physically _____

Spiritually _____

Socially _____

Courage Tools

What can I be thankful for?
Positivity _____

How do I say "stop," "no," "enough"?
Boundaries _____

Who do I need to forgive, including me?
Forgiveness _____

When or how can I confront this issue?
Confidence _____

What are the possibilities or opportunities?
Hope _____

Courage Challenge: What is something you can do or say differently today, which you have perhaps never done or done well before, that will challenge or change your broken pattern?

How do you feel about yourself and your life today?   **DATE:** _____

Emotionally _____

Mentally   _____

Physically   _____

Spiritually   _____

Socially   _____

Courage Tools

What can I be thankful for?
Positivity _____

How do I say "stop," "no," "enough"?
Boundaries _____

Who do I need to forgive, including me?
Forgiveness _____

When or how can I confront this issue?
Confidence _____

What are the possibilities or opportunities?
Hope _____

Courage Challenge: What is something you can do or say differently today, which you have perhaps never done or done well before, that will challenge or change your broken pattern?

How do you feel about yourself and your life today? **DATE:** _____

Emotionally _____
Mentally _____
Physically _____
Spiritually _____
Socially _____

Courage Tools

What can I be thankful for?
Positivity _____

How do I say "stop," "no," "enough"?
Boundaries _____

Who do I need to forgive, including me?
Forgiveness _____

When or how can I confront this issue?
Confidence _____

What are the possibilities or opportunities?
Hope _____

Courage Challenge: What is something you can do or say differently today, which you have perhaps never done or done well before, that will challenge or change your broken pattern?

How do you feel about yourself and your life today?   **DATE:** _____

Emotionally   _____

Mentally   _____

Physically   _____

Spiritually   _____

Socially   _____

Courage Tools

What can I be thankful for?
Positivity _____

How do I say "stop," "no," "enough"?
Boundaries _____

Who do I need to forgive, including me?
Forgiveness _____

When or how can I confront this issue?
Confidence _____

What are the possibilities or opportunities?
Hope _____

Courage Challenge: What is something you can do or say differently today, which you have perhaps never done or done well before, that will challenge or change your broken pattern?

How do you feel about yourself and your life today? **DATE:** _____

Emotionally _____

Mentally _____

Physically _____

Spiritually _____

Socially _____

Courage Tools

What can I be thankful for?
Positivity _____

How do I say "stop," "no," "enough"?
Boundaries _____

Who do I need to forgive, including me?
Forgiveness _____

When or how can I confront this issue?
Confidence _____

What are the possibilities or opportunities?
Hope _____

Courage Challenge: What is something you can do or say differently today, which you have perhaps never done or done well before, that will challenge or change your broken pattern?

How do you feel about yourself and your life today? **DATE:** _____

Emotionally _____

Mentally _____

Physically _____

Spiritually _____

Socially _____

Courage Tools

What can I be thankful for?
Positivity _____

How do I say "stop," "no," "enough"?
Boundaries _____

Who do I need to forgive, including me?
Forgiveness _____

When or how can I confront this issue?
Confidence _____

What are the possibilities or opportunities?
Hope _____

Courage Challenge: What is something you can do or say differently today, which you have perhaps never done or done well before, that will challenge or change your broken pattern?

How do you feel about yourself and your life today?   **DATE:** _____

Emotionally   _____

Mentally   _____

Physically   _____

Spiritually   _____

Socially   _____

Courage Tools

What can I be thankful for?
Positivity _____

How do I say "stop," "no," "enough"?
Boundaries _____

Who do I need to forgive, including me?
Forgiveness _____

When or how can I confront this issue?
Confidence _____

What are the possibilities or opportunities?
Hope _____

Courage Challenge: What is something you can do or say differently today, which you have perhaps never done or done well before, that will challenge or change your broken pattern?

Weekly Update..

From 1 to 10 with 10 being the best, how did you do this week with confronting, challenging or changing your broken patterns?

_____

Why did you do so well or so poorly?

_____

What is it going to take to get to the next level?

_____

> "What makes you different or weird, that's your strength."

– MERYL STREEP –

STRONGER DAYS

Because the first step to restoring your brokenness is admitting that you are broken, think about the aspect of your life that you most need to address this month:

_____

_____

_____

_____

_____

_____

_____

For the next several weeks, think about how you can confront and overcome your issue(s) by writing down your thoughts on the following pages each day.

How do you feel about yourself and your life today?   **DATE:** _____

Emotionally _____

Mentally _____

Physically _____

Spiritually _____

Socially _____

Courage Tools

What can I be thankful for?
Positivity _____

How do I say "stop," "no," "enough"?
Boundaries _____

Who do I need to forgive, including me?
Forgiveness _____

When or how can I confront this issue?
Confidence _____

What are the possibilities or opportunities?
Hope _____

Courage Challenge: What is something you can do or say differently today, which you have perhaps never done or done well before, that will challenge or change your broken pattern?

How do you feel about yourself and your life today? **DATE:** _____

Emotionally _____

Mentally _____

Physically _____

Spiritually _____

Socially _____

Courage Tools

What can I be thankful for?
Positivity _____

How do I say "stop," "no," "enough"?
Boundaries _____

Who do I need to forgive, including me?
Forgiveness _____

When or how can I confront this issue?
Confidence _____

What are the possibilities or opportunities?
Hope _____

Courage Challenge: What is something you can do or say differently today, which you have perhaps never done or done well before, that will challenge or change your broken pattern?

How do you feel about yourself and your life today?   **DATE:** _____

Emotionally _____

Mentally   _____

Physically   _____

Spiritually _____

Socially   _____

Courage Tools

What can I be thankful for?
Positivity _____

How do I say "stop," "no," "enough"?
Boundaries _____

Who do I need to forgive, including me?
Forgiveness _____

When or how can I confront this issue?
Confidence _____

What are the possibilities or opportunities?
Hope _____

Courage Challenge: What is something you can do or say differently today, which you have perhaps never done or done well before, that will challenge or change your broken pattern?

How do you feel about yourself and your life today? **DATE:** _____

Emotionally _____

Mentally _____

Physically _____

Spiritually _____

Socially _____

Courage Tools

What can I be thankful for?
Positivity _____

How do I say "stop," "no," "enough"?
Boundaries _____

Who do I need to forgive, including me?
Forgiveness _____

When or how can I confront this issue?
Confidence _____

What are the possibilities or opportunities?
Hope _____

Courage Challenge: What is something you can do or say differently today, which you have perhaps never done or done well before, that will challenge or change your broken pattern?

How do you feel about yourself and your life today?   **DATE:** _____

Emotionally   _____

Mentally   _____

Physically   _____

Spiritually   _____

Socially   _____

Courage Tools

What can I be thankful for?
Positivity _____

How do I say "stop," "no," "enough"?
Boundaries _____

Who do I need to forgive, including me?
Forgiveness _____

When or how can I confront this issue?
Confidence _____

What are the possibilities or opportunities?
Hope _____

Courage Challenge: What is something you can do or say differently today, which you have perhaps never done or done well before, that will challenge or change your broken pattern?

How do you feel about yourself and your life today?   **DATE:** _____

Emotionally _____

Mentally _____

Physically _____

Spiritually _____

Socially _____

Courage Tools

What can I be thankful for?
Positivity _____

How do I say "stop," "no," "enough"?
Boundaries _____

Who do I need to forgive, including me?
Forgiveness _____

When or how can I confront this issue?
Confidence _____

What are the possibilities or opportunities?
Hope _____

Courage Challenge: What is something you can do or say differently today, which you have perhaps never done or done well before, that will challenge or change your broken pattern?

How do you feel about yourself and your life today?   **DATE:** _____

Emotionally _____

Mentally _____

Physically _____

Spiritually _____

Socially _____

Courage Tools

What can I be thankful for?
Positivity _____

How do I say "stop," "no," "enough"?
Boundaries _____

Who do I need to forgive, including me?
Forgiveness _____

When or how can I confront this issue?
Confidence _____

What are the possibilities or opportunities?
Hope _____

Courage Challenge: What is something you can do or say differently today, which you have perhaps never done or done well before, that will challenge or change your broken pattern?

From 1 to 10 with 10 being the best, how did you do this week with confronting, challenging or changing your broken patterns?

_____

Why did you do so well or so poorly?

_____

What is it going to take to get to the next level?

_____

How do you feel about yourself and your life today? **DATE:** _____

Emotionally _____

Mentally _____

Physically _____

Spiritually _____

Socially _____

Courage Tools

What can I be thankful for?
Positivity _____

How do I say "stop," "no," "enough"?
Boundaries _____

Who do I need to forgive, including me?
Forgiveness _____

When or how can I confront this issue?
Confidence _____

What are the possibilities or opportunities?
Hope _____

Courage Challenge: What is something you can do or say differently today, which you have perhaps never done or done well before, that will challenge or change your broken pattern?

How do you feel about yourself and your life today? **DATE:** _____

Emotionally _____
Mentally   _____
Physically   _____
Spiritually _____
Socially   _____

Courage Tools

What can I be thankful for?
Positivity _____

How do I say "stop," "no," "enough"?
Boundaries _____

Who do I need to forgive, including me?
Forgiveness _____

When or how can I confront this issue?
Confidence _____

What are the possibilities or opportunities?
Hope _____

Courage Challenge: What is something you can do or say differently today, which you have perhaps never done or done well before, that will challenge or change your broken pattern?

How do you feel about yourself and your life today? **DATE:** _____

Emotionally _____

Mentally _____

Physically _____

Spiritually _____

Socially _____

Courage Tools

What can I be thankful for?
Positivity _____

How do I say "stop," "no," "enough"?
Boundaries _____

Who do I need to forgive, including me?
Forgiveness _____

When or how can I confront this issue?
Confidence _____

What are the possibilities or opportunities?
Hope _____

Courage Challenge: What is something you can do or say differently today, which you have perhaps never done or done well before, that will challenge or change your broken pattern?

How do you feel about yourself and your life today? **DATE:** _____

Emotionally _____
Mentally   _____
Physically   _____
Spiritually _____
Socially   _____

Courage Tools

What can I be thankful for?
Positivity _____

How do I say "stop," "no," "enough"?
Boundaries _____

Who do I need to forgive, including me?
Forgiveness _____

When or how can I confront this issue?
Confidence _____

What are the possibilities or opportunities?
Hope _____

Courage Challenge: What is something you can do or say differently today, which you have perhaps never done or done well before, that will challenge or change your broken pattern?

How do you feel about yourself and your life today?   **DATE:** _____

Emotionally _____

Mentally _____

Physically _____

Spiritually _____

Socially _____

Courage Tools

What can I be thankful for?
Positivity _____

How do I say "stop," "no," "enough"?
Boundaries _____

Who do I need to forgive, including me?
Forgiveness _____

When or how can I confront this issue?
Confidence _____

What are the possibilities or opportunities?
Hope _____

Courage Challenge: What is something you can do or say differently today, which you have perhaps never done or done well before, that will challenge or change your broken pattern?

How do you feel about yourself and your life today?   **DATE:** _____

Emotionally   _____

Mentally   _____

Physically   _____

Spiritually   _____

Socially   _____

Courage Tools

What can I be thankful for?
Positivity _____

How do I say "stop," "no," "enough"?
Boundaries _____

Who do I need to forgive, including me?
Forgiveness _____

When or how can I confront this issue?
Confidence _____

What are the possibilities or opportunities?
Hope _____

Courage Challenge: What is something you can do or say differently today, which you have perhaps never done or done well before, that will challenge or change your broken pattern?

How do you feel about yourself and your life today?   **DATE:** _____

Emotionally   _____

Mentally   _____

Physically   _____

Spiritually   _____

Socially   _____

Courage Tools

What can I be thankful for?
Positivity _____

How do I say "stop," "no," "enough"?
Boundaries _____

Who do I need to forgive, including me?
Forgiveness _____

When or how can I confront this issue?
Confidence _____

What are the possibilities or opportunities?
Hope _____

Courage Challenge: What is something you can do or say differently today, which you have perhaps never done or done well before, that will challenge or change your broken pattern?

From 1 to 10 with 10 being the best, how did you do this week with confronting, challenging or changing your broken patterns?

_____

Why did you do so well or so poorly?

_____

What is it going to take to get to the next level?

_____

How do you feel about yourself and your life today?   **DATE:** _____

Emotionally   _____

Mentally   _____

Physically   _____

Spiritually   _____

Socially   _____

Courage Tools

What can I be thankful for?
Positivity _____

How do I say "stop," "no," "enough"?
Boundaries _____

Who do I need to forgive, including me?
Forgiveness _____

When or how can I confront this issue?
Confidence _____

What are the possibilities or opportunities?
Hope _____

Courage Challenge: What is something you can do or say differently today, which you have perhaps never done or done well before, that will challenge or change your broken pattern?

How do you feel about yourself and your life today? **DATE:** _____

Emotionally _____

Mentally _____

Physically _____

Spiritually _____

Socially _____

Courage Tools

What can I be thankful for?
Positivity _____

How do I say "stop," "no," "enough"?
Boundaries _____

Who do I need to forgive, including me?
Forgiveness _____

When or how can I confront this issue?
Confidence _____

What are the possibilities or opportunities?
Hope _____

Courage Challenge: What is something you can do or say differently today, which you have perhaps never done or done well before, that will challenge or change your broken pattern?

How do you feel about yourself and your life today? **DATE:** _____

Emotionally _____

Mentally _____

Physically _____

Spiritually _____

Socially _____

Courage Tools

What can I be thankful for?
Positivity _____

How do I say "stop," "no," "enough"?
Boundaries _____

Who do I need to forgive, including me?
Forgiveness _____

When or how can I confront this issue?
Confidence _____

What are the possibilities or opportunities?
Hope _____

Courage Challenge: What is something you can do or say differently today, which you have perhaps never done or done well before, that will challenge or change your broken pattern?

How do you feel about yourself and your life today?   **DATE:** _____

Emotionally   _____

Mentally   _____

Physically   _____

Spiritually   _____

Socially   _____

Courage Tools

What can I be thankful for?
Positivity _____

How do I say "stop," "no," "enough"?
Boundaries _____

Who do I need to forgive, including me?
Forgiveness _____

When or how can I confront this issue?
Confidence _____

What are the possibilities or opportunities?
Hope _____

Courage Challenge: What is something you can do or say differently today, which you have perhaps never done or done well before, that will challenge or change your broken pattern?

How do you feel about yourself and your life today? **DATE:** _____

Emotionally _____

Mentally _____

Physically _____

Spiritually _____

Socially _____

Courage Tools

What can I be thankful for?
Positivity _____

How do I say "stop," "no," "enough"?
Boundaries _____

Who do I need to forgive, including me?
Forgiveness _____

When or how can I confront this issue?
Confidence _____

What are the possibilities or opportunities?
Hope _____

Courage Challenge: What is something you can do or say differently today, which you have perhaps never done or done well before, that will challenge or change your broken pattern?

How do you feel about yourself and your life today?   **DATE:** _____

Emotionally   _____

Mentally   _____

Physically   _____

Spiritually   _____

Socially   _____

Courage Tools

What can I be thankful for?
Positivity _____

How do I say "stop," "no," "enough"?
Boundaries _____

Who do I need to forgive, including me?
Forgiveness _____

When or how can I confront this issue?
Confidence _____

What are the possibilities or opportunities?
Hope _____

Courage Challenge: What is something you can do or say differently today, which you have perhaps never done or done well before, that will challenge or change your broken pattern?

How do you feel about yourself and your life today? **DATE:** _____

Emotionally _____

Mentally _____

Physically _____

Spiritually _____

Socially _____

Courage Tools

What can I be thankful for?
Positivity _____

How do I say "stop," "no," "enough"?
Boundaries _____

Who do I need to forgive, including me?
Forgiveness _____

When or how can I confront this issue?
Confidence _____

What are the possibilities or opportunities?
Hope _____

Courage Challenge: What is something you can do or say differently today, which you have perhaps never done or done well before, that will challenge or change your broken pattern?

From 1 to 10 with 10 being the best, how did you do this week with confronting, challenging or changing your broken patterns?

_____

Why did you do so well or so poorly?

_____

What is it going to take to get to the next level?

_____

How do you feel about yourself and your life today? **DATE:** _____

Emotionally _____
Mentally _____
Physically _____
Spiritually _____
Socially _____

Courage Tools

What can I be thankful for?
Positivity _____

How do I say "stop," "no," "enough"?
Boundaries _____

Who do I need to forgive, including me?
Forgiveness _____

When or how can I confront this issue?
Confidence _____

What are the possibilities or opportunities?
Hope _____

Courage Challenge: What is something you can do or say differently today, which you have perhaps never done or done well before, that will challenge or change your broken pattern?

How do you feel about yourself and your life today? **DATE:** _____

Emotionally _____

Mentally _____

Physically _____

Spiritually _____

Socially _____

Courage Tools

What can I be thankful for?
Positivity _____

How do I say "stop," "no," "enough"?
Boundaries _____

Who do I need to forgive, including me?
Forgiveness _____

When or how can I confront this issue?
Confidence _____

What are the possibilities or opportunities?
Hope _____

Courage Challenge: What is something you can do or say differently today, which you have perhaps never done or done well before, that will challenge or change your broken pattern?

How do you feel about yourself and your life today?   **DATE:** _____

Emotionally _____
Mentally   _____
Physically   _____
Spiritually _____
Socially   _____

Courage Tools

What can I be thankful for?
Positivity _____

How do I say "stop," "no," "enough"?
Boundaries _____

Who do I need to forgive, including me?
Forgiveness _____

When or how can I confront this issue?
Confidence _____

What are the possibilities or opportunities?
Hope _____

Courage Challenge: What is something you can do or say differently today, which you have perhaps never done or done well before, that will challenge or change your broken pattern?

How do you feel about yourself and your life today? **DATE:** _____

Emotionally _____

Mentally _____

Physically _____

Spiritually _____

Socially _____

Courage Tools

What can I be thankful for?
Positivity _____

How do I say "stop," "no," "enough"?
Boundaries _____

Who do I need to forgive, including me?
Forgiveness _____

When or how can I confront this issue?
Confidence _____

What are the possibilities or opportunities?
Hope _____

Courage Challenge: What is something you can do or say differently today, which you have perhaps never done or done well before, that will challenge or change your broken pattern?

How do you feel about yourself and your life today? **DATE:** _____

Emotionally _____

Mentally _____

Physically _____

Spiritually _____

Socially _____

Courage Tools

What can I be thankful for?
Positivity _____

How do I say "stop," "no," "enough"?
Boundaries _____

Who do I need to forgive, including me?
Forgiveness _____

When or how can I confront this issue?
Confidence _____

What are the possibilities or opportunities?
Hope _____

Courage Challenge: What is something you can do or say differently today, which you have perhaps never done or done well before, that will challenge or change your broken pattern?

How do you feel about yourself and your life today?　**DATE:** _____

Emotionally　_____

Mentally　_____

Physically　_____

Spiritually　_____

Socially　_____

Courage Tools

What can I be thankful for?
Positivity _____

How do I say "stop," "no," "enough"?
Boundaries _____

Who do I need to forgive, including me?
Forgiveness _____

When or how can I confront this issue?
Confidence _____

What are the possibilities or opportunities?
Hope _____

Courage Challenge: What is something you can do or say differently today, which you have perhaps never done or done well before, that will challenge or change your broken pattern?

How do you feel about yourself and your life today? **DATE:** _____

Emotionally _____

Mentally _____

Physically _____

Spiritually _____

Socially _____

Courage Tools

What can I be thankful for?
Positivity _____

How do I say "stop," "no," "enough"?
Boundaries _____

Who do I need to forgive, including me?
Forgiveness _____

When or how can I confront this issue?
Confidence _____

What are the possibilities or opportunities?
Hope _____

Courage Challenge: What is something you can do or say differently today, which you have perhaps never done or done well before, that will challenge or change your broken pattern?

UPDATE..

From 1 to 10 with 10 being the best, how did you do this week with confronting, challenging or changing your broken patterns?

_____

Why did you do so well or so poorly?

_____

What is it going to take to get to the next level?

_____

> "All you need is the plan, the road map, and the courage to press on to your destination."
>
> — EARL NIGHTINGALE —

STRONGER DAYS

Because the first step to restoring your brokenness is admitting that you are broken, think about the aspect of your life that you most need to address this month:

_____

_____

_____

_____

_____

_____

_____

For the next several weeks, think about how you can confront and overcome your issue(s) by writing down your thoughts on the following pages each day.

How do you feel about yourself and your life today? **DATE:** _____

Emotionally _____

Mentally _____

Physically _____

Spiritually _____

Socially _____

Courage Tools

What can I be thankful for?
Positivity _____

How do I say "stop," "no," "enough"?
Boundaries _____

Who do I need to forgive, including me?
Forgiveness _____

When or how can I confront this issue?
Confidence _____

What are the possibilities or opportunities?
Hope _____

Courage Challenge: What is something you can do or say differently today, which you have perhaps never done or done well before, that will challenge or change your broken pattern?

How do you feel about yourself and your life today? **DATE:** _____

Emotionally _____

Mentally _____

Physically _____

Spiritually _____

Socially _____

Courage Tools

What can I be thankful for?
Positivity _____

How do I say "stop," "no," "enough"?
Boundaries _____

Who do I need to forgive, including me?
Forgiveness _____

When or how can I confront this issue?
Confidence _____

What are the possibilities or opportunities?
Hope _____

Courage Challenge: What is something you can do or say differently today, which you have perhaps never done or done well before, that will challenge or change your broken pattern?

How do you feel about yourself and your life today? **DATE:** _____

Emotionally _____

Mentally _____

Physically _____

Spiritually _____

Socially _____

Courage Tools

What can I be thankful for?
Positivity _____

How do I say "stop," "no," "enough"?
Boundaries _____

Who do I need to forgive, including me?
Forgiveness _____

When or how can I confront this issue?
Confidence _____

What are the possibilities or opportunities?
Hope _____

Courage Challenge: What is something you can do or say differently today, which you have perhaps never done or done well before, that will challenge or change your broken pattern?

How do you feel about yourself and your life today? **DATE:** _____

Emotionally _____

Mentally _____

Physically _____

Spiritually _____

Socially _____

Courage Tools

What can I be thankful for?
Positivity _____

How do I say "stop," "no," "enough"?
Boundaries _____

Who do I need to forgive, including me?
Forgiveness _____

When or how can I confront this issue?
Confidence _____

What are the possibilities or opportunities?
Hope _____

Courage Challenge: What is something you can do or say differently today, which you have perhaps never done or done well before, that will challenge or change your broken pattern?

How do you feel about yourself and your life today?

DATE: _____

Emotionally _____

Mentally _____

Physically _____

Spiritually _____

Socially _____

Courage Tools

What can I be thankful for?
Positivity _____

How do I say "stop," "no," "enough"?
Boundaries _____

Who do I need to forgive, including me?
Forgiveness _____

When or how can I confront this issue?
Confidence _____

What are the possibilities or opportunities?
Hope _____

Courage Challenge: What is something you can do or say differently today, which you have perhaps never done or done well before, that will challenge or change your broken pattern?

How do you feel about yourself and your life today?

DATE: _____

Emotionally _____

Mentally _____

Physically _____

Spiritually _____

Socially _____

Courage Tools

What can I be thankful for?
Positivity _____

How do I say "stop," "no," "enough"?
Boundaries _____

Who do I need to forgive, including me?
Forgiveness _____

When or how can I confront this issue?
Confidence _____

What are the possibilities or opportunities?
Hope _____

Courage Challenge: What is something you can do or say differently today, which you have perhaps never done or done well before, that will challenge or change your broken pattern?

How do you feel about yourself and your life today?   **DATE:** _____

Emotionally _____

Mentally _____

Physically _____

Spiritually _____

Socially _____

Courage Tools

What can I be thankful for?
Positivity _____

How do I say "stop," "no," "enough"?
Boundaries _____

Who do I need to forgive, including me?
Forgiveness _____

When or how can I confront this issue?
Confidence _____

What are the possibilities or opportunities?
Hope _____

Courage Challenge: What is something you can do or say differently today, which you have perhaps never done or done well before, that will challenge or change your broken pattern?

Weekly
U P D A T E . .

From 1 to 10 with 10 being the best, how did you do this week with confronting, challenging or changing your broken patterns?

_____

Why did you do so well or so poorly?

_____

What is it going to take to get to the next level?

_____

How do you feel about yourself and your life today?   **DATE:** _____

Emotionally   _____

Mentally   _____

Physically   _____

Spiritually   _____

Socially   _____

Courage Tools

What can I be thankful for?
Positivity _____

How do I say "stop," "no," "enough"?
Boundaries _____

Who do I need to forgive, including me?
Forgiveness _____

When or how can I confront this issue?
Confidence _____

What are the possibilities or opportunities?
Hope _____

Courage Challenge: What is something you can do or say differently today, which you have perhaps never done or done well before, that will challenge or change your broken pattern?

How do you feel about yourself and your life today?   **DATE:** _____

Emotionally _____

Mentally _____

Physically _____

Spiritually _____

Socially _____

Courage Tools

What can I be thankful for?
Positivity _____

How do I say "stop," "no," "enough"?
Boundaries _____

Who do I need to forgive, including me?
Forgiveness _____

When or how can I confront this issue?
Confidence _____

What are the possibilities or opportunities?
Hope _____

Courage Challenge: What is something you can do or say differently today, which you have perhaps never done or done well before, that will challenge or change your broken pattern?

How do you feel about yourself and your life today?   **DATE:** _____

Emotionally _____

Mentally _____

Physically _____

Spiritually _____

Socially _____

Courage Tools

What can I be thankful for?
Positivity _____

How do I say "stop," "no," "enough"?
Boundaries _____

Who do I need to forgive, including me?
Forgiveness _____

When or how can I confront this issue?
Confidence _____

What are the possibilities or opportunities?
Hope _____

Courage Challenge: What is something you can do or say differently today, which you have perhaps never done or done well before, that will challenge or change your broken pattern?

How do you feel about yourself and your life today?   **DATE:** _____

Emotionally   _____

Mentally   _____

Physically   _____

Spiritually   _____

Socially   _____

Courage Tools

What can I be thankful for?
Positivity _____

How do I say "stop," "no," "enough"?
Boundaries _____

Who do I need to forgive, including me?
Forgiveness _____

When or how can I confront this issue?
Confidence _____

What are the possibilities or opportunities?
Hope _____

Courage Challenge: What is something you can do or say differently today, which you have perhaps never done or done well before, that will challenge or change your broken pattern?

How do you feel about yourself and your life today?   **DATE:** _____

Emotionally _____

Mentally _____

Physically _____

Spiritually _____

Socially _____

Courage Tools

What can I be thankful for?
Positivity _____

How do I say "stop," "no," "enough"?
Boundaries _____

Who do I need to forgive, including me?
Forgiveness _____

When or how can I confront this issue?
Confidence _____

What are the possibilities or opportunities?
Hope _____

Courage Challenge: What is something you can do or say differently today, which you have perhaps never done or done well before, that will challenge or change your broken pattern?

How do you feel about yourself and your life today? **DATE:** _____

Emotionally _____

Mentally _____

Physically _____

Spiritually _____

Socially _____

Courage Tools

What can I be thankful for?
Positivity _____

How do I say "stop," "no," "enough"?
Boundaries _____

Who do I need to forgive, including me?
Forgiveness _____

When or how can I confront this issue?
Confidence _____

What are the possibilities or opportunities?
Hope _____

Courage Challenge: What is something you can do or say differently today, which you have perhaps never done or done well before, that will challenge or change your broken pattern?

How do you feel about yourself and your life today? **DATE:** _____

Emotionally _____

Mentally   _____

Physically   _____

Spiritually _____

Socially   _____

Courage Tools

What can I be thankful for?
Positivity _____

How do I say "stop," "no," "enough"?
Boundaries _____

Who do I need to forgive, including me?
Forgiveness _____

When or how can I confront this issue?
Confidence _____

What are the possibilities or opportunities?
Hope _____

Courage Challenge: What is something you can do or say differently today, which you have perhaps never done or done well before, that will challenge or change your broken pattern?

From 1 to 10 with 10 being the best, how did you do this week with confronting, challenging or changing your broken patterns?

_____

Why did you do so well or so poorly?

_____

What is it going to take to get to the next level?

_____

How do you feel about yourself and your life today?   **DATE:** _____

Emotionally   _____

Mentally   _____

Physically   _____

Spiritually   _____

Socially   _____

Courage Tools

What can I be thankful for?
Positivity _____

How do I say "stop," "no," "enough"?
Boundaries _____

Who do I need to forgive, including me?
Forgiveness _____

When or how can I confront this issue?
Confidence _____

What are the possibilities or opportunities?
Hope _____

Courage Challenge: What is something you can do or say differently today, which you have perhaps never done or done well before, that will challenge or change your broken pattern?

How do you feel about yourself and your life today? **DATE:** _____

Emotionally _____

Mentally _____

Physically _____

Spiritually _____

Socially _____

Courage Tools

What can I be thankful for?
Positivity _____

How do I say "stop," "no," "enough"?
Boundaries _____

Who do I need to forgive, including me?
Forgiveness _____

When or how can I confront this issue?
Confidence _____

What are the possibilities or opportunities?
Hope _____

Courage Challenge: What is something you can do or say differently today, which you have perhaps never done or done well before, that will challenge or change your broken pattern?

How do you feel about yourself and your life today?   **DATE:** _____

Emotionally _____

Mentally   _____

Physically   _____

Spiritually _____

Socially   _____

Courage Tools

What can I be thankful for?
Positivity _____

How do I say "stop," "no," "enough"?
Boundaries _____

Who do I need to forgive, including me?
Forgiveness _____

When or how can I confront this issue?
Confidence _____

What are the possibilities or opportunities?
Hope _____

Courage Challenge: What is something you can do or say differently today, which you have perhaps never done or done well before, that will challenge or change your broken pattern?

How do you feel about yourself and your life today? **DATE:** _____

Emotionally _____

Mentally _____

Physically _____

Spiritually _____

Socially _____

Courage Tools

What can I be thankful for?
Positivity _____

How do I say "stop," "no," "enough"?
Boundaries _____

Who do I need to forgive, including me?
Forgiveness _____

When or how can I confront this issue?
Confidence _____

What are the possibilities or opportunities?
Hope _____

Courage Challenge: What is something you can do or say differently today, which you have perhaps never done or done well before, that will challenge or change your broken pattern?

How do you feel about yourself and your life today? **DATE:** _____

Emotionally _____

Mentally _____

Physically _____

Spiritually _____

Socially _____

Courage Tools

What can I be thankful for?
Positivity _____

How do I say "stop," "no," "enough"?
Boundaries _____

Who do I need to forgive, including me?
Forgiveness _____

When or how can I confront this issue?
Confidence _____

What are the possibilities or opportunities?
Hope _____

Courage Challenge: What is something you can do or say differently today, which you have perhaps never done or done well before, that will challenge or change your broken pattern?

How do you feel about yourself and your life today?   **DATE:** _____

Emotionally _____

Mentally   _____

Physically   _____

Spiritually _____

Socially   _____

Courage Tools

What can I be thankful for?
Positivity _____

How do I say "stop," "no," "enough"?
Boundaries _____

Who do I need to forgive, including me?
Forgiveness _____

When or how can I confront this issue?
Confidence _____

What are the possibilities or opportunities?
Hope _____

Courage Challenge: What is something you can do or say differently today, which you have perhaps never done or done well before, that will challenge or change your broken pattern?

How do you feel about yourself and your life today?   **DATE:** _____

Emotionally _____

Mentally   _____

Physically   _____

Spiritually _____

Socially   _____

Courage Tools

What can I be thankful for?
Positivity _____

How do I say "stop," "no," "enough"?
Boundaries _____

Who do I need to forgive, including me?
Forgiveness _____

When or how can I confront this issue?
Confidence _____

What are the possibilities or opportunities?
Hope _____

Courage Challenge: What is something you can do or say differently today, which you have perhaps never done or done well before, that will challenge or change your broken pattern?

Weekly
U P D A T E . .

From 1 to 10 with 10 being the best, how did you do this week with confronting, challenging or changing your broken patterns?

_____

Why did you do so well or so poorly?

_____

What is it going to take to get to the next level?

_____

How do you feel about yourself and your life today?   **DATE:** _____

Emotionally   _____

Mentally   _____

Physically   _____

Spiritually   _____

Socially   _____

Courage Tools

What can I be thankful for?
Positivity _____

How do I say "stop," "no," "enough"?
Boundaries _____

Who do I need to forgive, including me?
Forgiveness _____

When or how can I confront this issue?
Confidence _____

What are the possibilities or opportunities?
Hope _____

Courage Challenge: What is something you can do or say differently today, which you have perhaps never done or done well before, that will challenge or change your broken pattern?

How do you feel about yourself and your life today?   **DATE:** _____

Emotionally _____

Mentally _____

Physically _____

Spiritually _____

Socially _____

Courage Tools

What can I be thankful for?
Positivity _____

How do I say "stop," "no," "enough"?
Boundaries _____

Who do I need to forgive, including me?
Forgiveness _____

When or how can I confront this issue?
Confidence _____

What are the possibilities or opportunities?
Hope _____

Courage Challenge: What is something you can do or say differently today, which you have perhaps never done or done well before, that will challenge or change your broken pattern?

How do you feel about yourself and your life today? **DATE:** _____

Emotionally _____

Mentally _____

Physically _____

Spiritually _____

Socially _____

Courage Tools

What can I be thankful for?
Positivity _____

How do I say "stop," "no," "enough"?
Boundaries _____

Who do I need to forgive, including me?
Forgiveness _____

When or how can I confront this issue?
Confidence _____

What are the possibilities or opportunities?
Hope _____

Courage Challenge: What is something you can do or say differently today, which you have perhaps never done or done well before, that will challenge or change your broken pattern?

How do you feel about yourself and your life today?   **DATE:** _____

Emotionally   _____

Mentally   _____

Physically   _____

Spiritually   _____

Socially   _____

Courage Tools

What can I be thankful for?
Positivity _____

How do I say "stop," "no," "enough"?
Boundaries _____

Who do I need to forgive, including me?
Forgiveness _____

When or how can I confront this issue?
Confidence _____

What are the possibilities or opportunities?
Hope _____

Courage Challenge: What is something you can do or say differently today, which you have perhaps never done or done well before, that will challenge or change your broken pattern?

How do you feel about yourself and your life today? **DATE:** _____

Emotionally   _____

Mentally   _____

Physically   _____

Spiritually   _____

Socially   _____

Courage Tools

What can I be thankful for?
Positivity _____

How do I say "stop," "no," "enough"?
Boundaries _____

Who do I need to forgive, including me?
Forgiveness _____

When or how can I confront this issue?
Confidence _____

What are the possibilities or opportunities?
Hope _____

Courage Challenge: What is something you can do or say differently today, which you have perhaps never done or done well before, that will challenge or change your broken pattern?

How do you feel about yourself and your life today?   **DATE:** _____

Emotionally   _____

Mentally   _____

Physically   _____

Spiritually   _____

Socially   _____

Courage Tools

What can I be thankful for?
Positivity _____

How do I say "stop," "no," "enough"?
Boundaries _____

Who do I need to forgive, including me?
Forgiveness _____

When or how can I confront this issue?
Confidence _____

What are the possibilities or opportunities?
Hope _____

Courage Challenge: What is something you can do or say differently today, which you have perhaps never done or done well before, that will challenge or change your broken pattern?

How do you feel about yourself and your life today?   **DATE:** _____

Emotionally _____

Mentally _____

Physically _____

Spiritually _____

Socially _____

Courage Tools

What can I be thankful for?
Positivity _____

How do I say "stop," "no," "enough"?
Boundaries _____

Who do I need to forgive, including me?
Forgiveness _____

When or how can I confront this issue?
Confidence _____

What are the possibilities or opportunities?
Hope _____

Courage Challenge: What is something you can do or say differently today, which you have perhaps never done or done well before, that will challenge or change your broken pattern?

Weekly
U P D A T E . .

From 1 to 10 with 10 being the best, how did you do this week with confronting, challenging or changing your broken patterns?

_____

Why did you do so well or so poorly?

_____

What is it going to take to get to the next level?

_____

> "All our dreams can come true if we have the courage to pursue them."

— WALT DISNEY —

STRONGER DAYS

Because the first step to restoring your brokenness is admitting that you are broken, think about the aspect of your life that you most need to address this month:

_____

_____

_____

_____

_____

_____

_____

For the next several weeks, think about how you can confront and overcome your issue(s) by writing down your thoughts on the following pages each day.

How do you feel about yourself and your life today?   **DATE:** _____

Emotionally _____

Mentally   _____

Physically   _____

Spiritually _____

Socially   _____

Courage Tools

What can I be thankful for?
Positivity _____

How do I say "stop," "no," "enough"?
Boundaries _____

Who do I need to forgive, including me?
Forgiveness _____

When or how can I confront this issue?
Confidence _____

What are the possibilities or opportunities?
Hope _____

Courage Challenge: What is something you can do or say differently today, which you have perhaps never done or done well before, that will challenge or change your broken pattern?

How do you feel about yourself and your life today?   **DATE:** _____

Emotionally   _____

Mentally   _____

Physically   _____

Spiritually   _____

Socially   _____

Courage Tools

What can I be thankful for?
Positivity _____

How do I say "stop," "no," "enough"?
Boundaries _____

Who do I need to forgive, including me?
Forgiveness _____

When or how can I confront this issue?
Confidence _____

What are the possibilities or opportunities?
Hope _____

Courage Challenge: What is something you can do or say differently today, which you have perhaps never done or done well before, that will challenge or change your broken pattern?

How do you feel about yourself and your life today?   **DATE:** _____

Emotionally _____

Mentally _____

Physically _____

Spiritually _____

Socially _____

Courage Tools

What can I be thankful for?
Positivity _____

How do I say "stop," "no," "enough"?
Boundaries _____

Who do I need to forgive, including me?
Forgiveness _____

When or how can I confront this issue?
Confidence _____

What are the possibilities or opportunities?
Hope _____

Courage Challenge: What is something you can do or say differently today, which you have perhaps never done or done well before, that will challenge or change your broken pattern?

How do you feel about yourself and your life today?   **DATE:** _____

Emotionally   _____

Mentally   _____

Physically   _____

Spiritually   _____

Socially   _____

Courage Tools

What can I be thankful for?
Positivity _____

How do I say "stop," "no," "enough"?
Boundaries _____

Who do I need to forgive, including me?
Forgiveness _____

When or how can I confront this issue?
Confidence _____

What are the possibilities or opportunities?
Hope _____

Courage Challenge: What is something you can do or say differently today, which you have perhaps never done or done well before, that will challenge or change your broken pattern?

How do you feel about yourself and your life today? **DATE:** _____

Emotionally _____

Mentally _____

Physically _____

Spiritually _____

Socially _____

Courage Tools

What can I be thankful for?
Positivity _____

How do I say "stop," "no," "enough"?
Boundaries _____

Who do I need to forgive, including me?
Forgiveness _____

When or how can I confront this issue?
Confidence _____

What are the possibilities or opportunities?
Hope _____

Courage Challenge: What is something you can do or say differently today, which you have perhaps never done or done well before, that will challenge or change your broken pattern?

How do you feel about yourself and your life today? **DATE:** _____

Emotionally _____

Mentally _____

Physically _____

Spiritually _____

Socially _____

Courage Tools

What can I be thankful for?
Positivity _____

How do I say "stop," "no," "enough"?
Boundaries _____

Who do I need to forgive, including me?
Forgiveness _____

When or how can I confront this issue?
Confidence _____

What are the possibilities or opportunities?
Hope _____

Courage Challenge: What is something you can do or say differently today, which you have perhaps never done or done well before, that will challenge or change your broken pattern?

How do you feel about yourself and your life today? **DATE:** _____

Emotionally _____

Mentally _____

Physically _____

Spiritually _____

Socially _____

Courage Tools

What can I be thankful for?
Positivity _____

How do I say "stop," "no," "enough"?
Boundaries _____

Who do I need to forgive, including me?
Forgiveness _____

When or how can I confront this issue?
Confidence _____

What are the possibilities or opportunities?
Hope _____

Courage Challenge: What is something you can do or say differently today, which you have perhaps never done or done well before, that will challenge or change your broken pattern?

Weekly
U P D A T E . .

From 1 to 10 with 10 being the best, how did you do this week with confronting, challenging or changing your broken patterns?

_____

Why did you do so well or so poorly?

_____

What is it going to take to get to the next level?

_____

How do you feel about yourself and your life today? **DATE:** _____

Emotionally _____

Mentally _____

Physically _____

Spiritually _____

Socially _____

Courage Tools

What can I be thankful for?
Positivity _____

How do I say "stop," "no," "enough"?
Boundaries _____

Who do I need to forgive, including me?
Forgiveness _____

When or how can I confront this issue?
Confidence _____

What are the possibilities or opportunities?
Hope _____

Courage Challenge: What is something you can do or say differently today, which you have perhaps never done or done well before, that will challenge or change your broken pattern?

How do you feel about yourself and your life today? **DATE:** _____

Emotionally _____

Mentally _____

Physically _____

Spiritually _____

Socially _____

Courage Tools

What can I be thankful for?
Positivity _____

How do I say "stop," "no," "enough"?
Boundaries _____

Who do I need to forgive, including me?
Forgiveness _____

When or how can I confront this issue?
Confidence _____

What are the possibilities or opportunities?
Hope _____

Courage Challenge: What is something you can do or say differently today, which you have perhaps never done or done well before, that will challenge or change your broken pattern?

How do you feel about yourself and your life today? **DATE:** _____

Emotionally _____

Mentally _____

Physically _____

Spiritually _____

Socially _____

Courage Tools

What can I be thankful for?
Positivity _____

How do I say "stop," "no," "enough"?
Boundaries _____

Who do I need to forgive, including me?
Forgiveness _____

When or how can I confront this issue?
Confidence _____

What are the possibilities or opportunities?
Hope _____

Courage Challenge: What is something you can do or say differently today, which you have perhaps never done or done well before, that will challenge or change your broken pattern?

How do you feel about yourself and your life today?   **DATE:** _____

Emotionally   _____

Mentally   _____

Physically   _____

Spiritually   _____

Socially   _____

Courage Tools

What can I be thankful for?
Positivity _____

How do I say "stop," "no," "enough"?
Boundaries _____

Who do I need to forgive, including me?
Forgiveness _____

When or how can I confront this issue?
Confidence _____

What are the possibilities or opportunities?
Hope _____

Courage Challenge: What is something you can do or say differently today, which you have perhaps never done or done well before, that will challenge or change your broken pattern?

How do you feel about yourself and your life today?   **DATE:** _____

Emotionally   _____

Mentally   _____

Physically   _____

Spiritually   _____

Socially   _____

Courage Tools

What can I be thankful for?
Positivity _____

How do I say "stop," "no," "enough"?
Boundaries _____

Who do I need to forgive, including me?
Forgiveness _____

When or how can I confront this issue?
Confidence _____

What are the possibilities or opportunities?
Hope _____

Courage Challenge: What is something you can do or say differently today, which you have perhaps never done or done well before, that will challenge or change your broken pattern?

How do you feel about yourself and your life today? **DATE:** _____

Emotionally _____
Mentally _____
Physically _____
Spiritually _____
Socially _____

Courage Tools

What can I be thankful for?
Positivity _____

How do I say "stop," "no," "enough"?
Boundaries _____

Who do I need to forgive, including me?
Forgiveness _____

When or how can I confront this issue?
Confidence _____

What are the possibilities or opportunities?
Hope _____

Courage Challenge: What is something you can do or say differently today, which you have perhaps never done or done well before, that will challenge or change your broken pattern?

How do you feel about yourself and your life today?   **DATE:** _____

Emotionally   _____

Mentally   _____

Physically   _____

Spiritually   _____

Socially   _____

Courage Tools

What can I be thankful for?
Positivity _____

How do I say "stop," "no," "enough"?
Boundaries _____

Who do I need to forgive, including me?
Forgiveness _____

When or how can I confront this issue?
Confidence _____

What are the possibilities or opportunities?
Hope _____

Courage Challenge: What is something you can do or say differently today, which you have perhaps never done or done well before, that will challenge or change your broken pattern?

UPDATE..

From 1 to 10 with 10 being the best, how did you do this week with confronting, challenging or changing your broken patterns?

_____

Why did you do so well or so poorly?

_____

What is it going to take to get to the next level?

_____

How do you feel about yourself and your life today?   **DATE:** _____

Emotionally _____

Mentally _____

Physically _____

Spiritually _____

Socially _____

Courage Tools

What can I be thankful for?
Positivity _____

How do I say "stop," "no," "enough"?
Boundaries _____

Who do I need to forgive, including me?
Forgiveness _____

When or how can I confront this issue?
Confidence _____

What are the possibilities or opportunities?
Hope _____

Courage Challenge: What is something you can do or say differently today, which you have perhaps never done or done well before, that will challenge or change your broken pattern?

DATE: _____

How do you feel about yourself and your life today?

Emotionally _____

Mentally _____

Physically _____

Spiritually _____

Socially _____

Courage Tools

What can I be thankful for?
Positivity _____

How do I say "stop," "no," "enough"?
Boundaries _____

Who do I need to forgive, including me?
Forgiveness _____

When or how can I confront this issue?
Confidence _____

What are the possibilities or opportunities?
Hope _____

Courage Challenge: What is something you can do or say differently today, which you have perhaps never done or done well before, that will challenge or change your broken pattern?

How do you feel about yourself and your life today? **DATE:** _____

Emotionally _____

Mentally _____

Physically _____

Spiritually _____

Socially _____

Courage Tools

What can I be thankful for?
Positivity _____

How do I say "stop," "no," "enough"?
Boundaries _____

Who do I need to forgive, including me?
Forgiveness _____

When or how can I confront this issue?
Confidence _____

What are the possibilities or opportunities?
Hope _____

Courage Challenge: What is something you can do or say differently today, which you have perhaps never done or done well before, that will challenge or change your broken pattern?

How do you feel about yourself and your life today? **DATE:** _____

Emotionally _____

Mentally _____

Physically _____

Spiritually _____

Socially _____

Courage Tools

What can I be thankful for?
Positivity _____

How do I say "stop," "no," "enough"?
Boundaries _____

Who do I need to forgive, including me?
Forgiveness _____

When or how can I confront this issue?
Confidence _____

What are the possibilities or opportunities?
Hope _____

Courage Challenge: What is something you can do or say differently today, which you have perhaps never done or done well before, that will challenge or change your broken pattern?

How do you feel about yourself and your life today?   **DATE:**

Emotionally _____

Mentally _____

Physically _____

Spiritually _____

Socially _____

Courage Tools

What can I be thankful for?
Positivity _____

How do I say "stop," "no," "enough"?
Boundaries _____

Who do I need to forgive, including me?
Forgiveness _____

When or how can I confront this issue?
Confidence _____

What are the possibilities or opportunities?
Hope _____

Courage Challenge: What is something you can do or say differently today, which you have perhaps never done or done well before, that will challenge or change your broken pattern?

How do you feel about yourself and your life today?   **DATE:** _____

Emotionally   _____

Mentally   _____

Physically   _____

Spiritually   _____

Socially   _____

Courage Tools

What can I be thankful for?
Positivity _____

How do I say "stop," "no," "enough"?
Boundaries _____

Who do I need to forgive, including me?
Forgiveness _____

When or how can I confront this issue?
Confidence _____

What are the possibilities or opportunities?
Hope _____

Courage Challenge: What is something you can do or say differently today, which you have perhaps never done or done well before, that will challenge or change your broken pattern?

How do you feel about yourself and your life today?   **DATE:** _____

Emotionally   _____

Mentally   _____

Physically   _____

Spiritually   _____

Socially   _____

Courage Tools

What can I be thankful for?
Positivity _____

How do I say "stop," "no," "enough"?
Boundaries _____

Who do I need to forgive, including me?
Forgiveness _____

When or how can I confront this issue?
Confidence _____

What are the possibilities or opportunities?
Hope _____

Courage Challenge: What is something you can do or say differently today, which you have perhaps never done or done well before, that will challenge or change your broken pattern?

UPDATE..

From 1 to 10 with 10 being the best, how did you do this week with confronting, challenging or changing your broken patterns?

_____

Why did you do so well or so poorly?

_____

What is it going to take to get to the next level?

_____

How do you feel about yourself and your life today? **DATE:** _____

Emotionally _____

Mentally _____

Physically _____

Spiritually _____

Socially _____

Courage Tools

What can I be thankful for?
Positivity _____

How do I say "stop," "no," "enough"?
Boundaries _____

Who do I need to forgive, including me?
Forgiveness _____

When or how can I confront this issue?
Confidence _____

What are the possibilities or opportunities?
Hope _____

Courage Challenge: What is something you can do or say differently today, which you have perhaps never done or done well before, that will challenge or change your broken pattern?

How do you feel about yourself and your life today? **DATE:** _____

Emotionally _____

Mentally _____

Physically _____

Spiritually _____

Socially _____

Courage Tools

What can I be thankful for?
Positivity _____

How do I say "stop," "no," "enough"?
Boundaries _____

Who do I need to forgive, including me?
Forgiveness _____

When or how can I confront this issue?
Confidence _____

What are the possibilities or opportunities?
Hope _____

Courage Challenge: What is something you can do or say differently today, which you have perhaps never done or done well before, that will challenge or change your broken pattern?

How do you feel about yourself and your life today?   **DATE:** _____

Emotionally _____

Mentally _____

Physically _____

Spiritually _____

Socially _____

Courage Tools

What can I be thankful for?
Positivity _____

How do I say "stop," "no," "enough"?
Boundaries _____

Who do I need to forgive, including me?
Forgiveness _____

When or how can I confront this issue?
Confidence _____

What are the possibilities or opportunities?
Hope _____

Courage Challenge: What is something you can do or say differently today, which you have perhaps never done or done well before, that will challenge or change your broken pattern?

How do you feel about yourself and your life today? **DATE:** _____

Emotionally _____

Mentally _____

Physically _____

Spiritually _____

Socially _____

Courage Tools

What can I be thankful for?
Positivity _____

How do I say "stop," "no," "enough"?
Boundaries _____

Who do I need to forgive, including me?
Forgiveness _____

When or how can I confront this issue?
Confidence _____

What are the possibilities or opportunities?
Hope _____

Courage Challenge: What is something you can do or say differently today, which you have perhaps never done or done well before, that will challenge or change your broken pattern?

How do you feel about yourself and your life today? **DATE:** _____

Emotionally _____

Mentally _____

Physically _____

Spiritually _____

Socially _____

Courage Tools

What can I be thankful for?
Positivity _____

How do I say "stop," "no," "enough"?
Boundaries _____

Who do I need to forgive, including me?
Forgiveness _____

When or how can I confront this issue?
Confidence _____

What are the possibilities or opportunities?
Hope _____

Courage Challenge: What is something you can do or say differently today, which you have perhaps never done or done well before, that will challenge or change your broken pattern?

How do you feel about yourself and your life today?   **DATE:** _____

Emotionally _____

Mentally _____

Physically _____

Spiritually _____

Socially _____

Courage Tools

What can I be thankful for?
Positivity _____

How do I say "stop," "no," "enough"?
Boundaries _____

Who do I need to forgive, including me?
Forgiveness _____

When or how can I confront this issue?
Confidence _____

What are the possibilities or opportunities?
Hope _____

Courage Challenge: What is something you can do or say differently today, which you have perhaps never done or done well before, that will challenge or change your broken pattern?

How do you feel about yourself and your life today? **DATE:** _____

Emotionally _____

Mentally _____

Physically _____

Spiritually _____

Socially _____

Courage Tools

What can I be thankful for?
Positivity _____

How do I say "stop," "no," "enough"?
Boundaries _____

Who do I need to forgive, including me?
Forgiveness _____

When or how can I confront this issue?
Confidence _____

What are the possibilities or opportunities?
Hope _____

Courage Challenge: What is something you can do or say differently today, which you have perhaps never done or done well before, that will challenge or change your broken pattern?

From 1 to 10 with 10 being the best, how did you do this week with confronting, challenging or changing your broken patterns?

_____

Why did you do so well or so poorly?

_____

What is it going to take to get to the next level?

_____

> "The undertaking of a new action brings new strength."

— RICHARD L. EVANS —

STRONGER DAYS

Because the first step to restoring your brokenness is admitting that you are broken, think about the aspect of your life that you most need to address this month:

_____

_____

_____

_____

_____

_____

_____

For the next several weeks, think about how you can confront and overcome your issue(s) by writing down your thoughts on the following pages each day.

How do you feel about yourself and your life today?   **DATE:** _____

Emotionally   _____

Mentally   _____

Physically   _____

Spiritually   _____

Socially   _____

Courage Tools

What can I be thankful for?
Positivity _____

How do I say "stop," "no," "enough"?
Boundaries _____

Who do I need to forgive, including me?
Forgiveness _____

When or how can I confront this issue?
Confidence _____

What are the possibilities or opportunities?
Hope _____

Courage Challenge: What is something you can do or say differently today, which you have perhaps never done or done well before, that will challenge or change your broken pattern?

How do you feel about yourself and your life today? **DATE:** _____

Emotionally _____

Mentally _____

Physically _____

Spiritually _____

Socially _____

Courage Tools

What can I be thankful for?
Positivity _____

How do I say "stop," "no," "enough"?
Boundaries _____

Who do I need to forgive, including me?
Forgiveness _____

When or how can I confront this issue?
Confidence _____

What are the possibilities or opportunities?
Hope _____

Courage Challenge: What is something you can do or say differently today, which you have perhaps never done or done well before, that will challenge or change your broken pattern?

How do you feel about yourself and your life today?   **DATE:** _____

Emotionally   _____

Mentally   _____

Physically   _____

Spiritually   _____

Socially   _____

Courage Tools

What can I be thankful for?
Positivity _____

How do I say "stop," "no," "enough"?
Boundaries _____

Who do I need to forgive, including me?
Forgiveness _____

When or how can I confront this issue?
Confidence _____

What are the possibilities or opportunities?
Hope _____

Courage Challenge: What is something you can do or say differently today, which you have perhaps never done or done well before, that will challenge or change your broken pattern?

How do you feel about yourself and your life today?   **DATE:** _____

Emotionally _____

Mentally   _____

Physically   _____

Spiritually _____

Socially   _____

Courage Tools

What can I be thankful for?
Positivity _____

How do I say "stop," "no," "enough"?
Boundaries _____

Who do I need to forgive, including me?
Forgiveness _____

When or how can I confront this issue?
Confidence _____

What are the possibilities or opportunities?
Hope _____

Courage Challenge: What is something you can do or say differently today, which you have perhaps never done or done well before, that will challenge or change your broken pattern?

How do you feel about yourself and your life today?   **DATE:** _____

Emotionally   _____

Mentally   _____

Physically   _____

Spiritually   _____

Socially   _____

Courage Tools

What can I be thankful for?
Positivity _____

How do I say "stop," "no," "enough"?
Boundaries _____

Who do I need to forgive, including me?
Forgiveness _____

When or how can I confront this issue?
Confidence _____

What are the possibilities or opportunities?
Hope _____

Courage Challenge: What is something you can do or say differently today, which you have perhaps never done or done well before, that will challenge or change your broken pattern?

How do you feel about yourself and your life today?   **DATE:** _____

Emotionally   _____

Mentally   _____

Physically   _____

Spiritually   _____

Socially   _____

Courage Tools

What can I be thankful for?
Positivity _____

How do I say "stop," "no," "enough"?
Boundaries _____

Who do I need to forgive, including me?
Forgiveness _____

When or how can I confront this issue?
Confidence _____

What are the possibilities or opportunities?
Hope _____

Courage Challenge: What is something you can do or say differently today, which you have perhaps never done or done well before, that will challenge or change your broken pattern?

How do you feel about yourself and your life today? **DATE:** _____

Emotionally _____

Mentally _____

Physically _____

Spiritually _____

Socially _____

Courage Tools

What can I be thankful for?
Positivity _____

How do I say "stop," "no," "enough"?
Boundaries _____

Who do I need to forgive, including me?
Forgiveness _____

When or how can I confront this issue?
Confidence _____

What are the possibilities or opportunities?
Hope _____

Courage Challenge: What is something you can do or say differently today, which you have perhaps never done or done well before, that will challenge or change your broken pattern?

Weekly
U P D A T E . .

From 1 to 10 with 10 being the best, how did you do this week with confronting, challenging or changing your broken patterns?

_____

Why did you do so well or so poorly?

_____

What is it going to take to get to the next level?

_____

How do you feel about yourself and your life today? **DATE:** _____

Emotionally _____

Mentally _____

Physically _____

Spiritually _____

Socially _____

Courage Tools

What can I be thankful for?
Positivity _____

How do I say "stop," "no," "enough"?
Boundaries _____

Who do I need to forgive, including me?
Forgiveness _____

When or how can I confront this issue?
Confidence _____

What are the possibilities or opportunities?
Hope _____

Courage Challenge: What is something you can do or say differently today, which you have perhaps never done or done well before, that will challenge or change your broken pattern?

How do you feel about yourself and your life today? **DATE:** _____

Emotionally _____

Mentally _____

Physically _____

Spiritually _____

Socially _____

Courage Tools

What can I be thankful for?
Positivity _____

How do I say "stop," "no," "enough"?
Boundaries _____

Who do I need to forgive, including me?
Forgiveness _____

When or how can I confront this issue?
Confidence _____

What are the possibilities or opportunities?
Hope _____

Courage Challenge: What is something you can do or say differently today, which you have perhaps never done or done well before, that will challenge or change your broken pattern?

How do you feel about yourself and your life today?   **DATE:** _____

Emotionally _____

Mentally   _____

Physically   _____

Spiritually _____

Socially   _____

Courage Tools

What can I be thankful for?
Positivity _____

How do I say "stop," "no," "enough"?
Boundaries _____

Who do I need to forgive, including me?
Forgiveness _____

When or how can I confront this issue?
Confidence _____

What are the possibilities or opportunities?
Hope _____

Courage Challenge: What is something you can do or say differently today, which you have perhaps never done or done well before, that will challenge or change your broken pattern?

DATE: _____

How do you feel about yourself and your life today?

Emotionally _____

Mentally   _____

Physically   _____

Spiritually   _____

Socially   _____

Courage Tools

What can I be thankful for?
Positivity _____

How do I say "stop," "no," "enough"?
Boundaries _____

Who do I need to forgive, including me?
Forgiveness _____

When or how can I confront this issue?
Confidence _____

What are the possibilities or opportunities?
Hope _____

Courage Challenge: What is something you can do or say differently today, which you have perhaps never done or done well before, that will challenge or change your broken pattern?

How do you feel about yourself and your life today? **DATE:** _____

Emotionally _____

Mentally _____

Physically _____

Spiritually _____

Socially _____

Courage Tools

What can I be thankful for?
Positivity _____

How do I say "stop," "no," "enough"?
Boundaries _____

Who do I need to forgive, including me?
Forgiveness _____

When or how can I confront this issue?
Confidence _____

What are the possibilities or opportunities?
Hope _____

Courage Challenge: What is something you can do or say differently today, which you have perhaps never done or done well before, that will challenge or change your broken pattern?

How do you feel about yourself and your life today?   **DATE:** _____

Emotionally   _____
Mentally   _____
Physically   _____
Spiritually   _____
Socially   _____

Courage Tools

What can I be thankful for?
Positivity _____

How do I say "stop," "no," "enough"?
Boundaries _____

Who do I need to forgive, including me?
Forgiveness _____

When or how can I confront this issue?
Confidence _____

What are the possibilities or opportunities?
Hope _____

Courage Challenge: What is something you can do or say differently today, which you have perhaps never done or done well before, that will challenge or change your broken pattern?

How do you feel about yourself and your life today?   **DATE:** _____

Emotionally _____

Mentally _____

Physically _____

Spiritually _____

Socially _____

Courage Tools

What can I be thankful for?
Positivity _____

How do I say "stop," "no," "enough"?
Boundaries _____

Who do I need to forgive, including me?
Forgiveness _____

When or how can I confront this issue?
Confidence _____

What are the possibilities or opportunities?
Hope _____

Courage Challenge: What is something you can do or say differently today, which you have perhaps never done or done well before, that will challenge or change your broken pattern?

From 1 to 10 with 10 being the best, how did you do this week with confronting, challenging or changing your broken patterns?

_____

Why did you do so well or so poorly?

_____

What is it going to take to get to the next level?

_____

How do you feel about yourself and your life today? **DATE:** _____

Emotionally _____

Mentally _____

Physically _____

Spiritually _____

Socially _____

Courage Tools

What can I be thankful for?
Positivity _____

How do I say "stop," "no," "enough"?
Boundaries _____

Who do I need to forgive, including me?
Forgiveness _____

When or how can I confront this issue?
Confidence _____

What are the possibilities or opportunities?
Hope _____

Courage Challenge: What is something you can do or say differently today, which you have perhaps never done or done well before, that will challenge or change your broken pattern?

How do you feel about yourself and your life today?   **DATE:** _____

Emotionally _____

Mentally _____

Physically _____

Spiritually _____

Socially _____

Courage Tools

What can I be thankful for?
Positivity _____

How do I say "stop," "no," "enough"?
Boundaries _____

Who do I need to forgive, including me?
Forgiveness _____

When or how can I confront this issue?
Confidence _____

What are the possibilities or opportunities?
Hope _____

Courage Challenge: What is something you can do or say differently today, which you have perhaps never done or done well before, that will challenge or change your broken pattern?

How do you feel about yourself and your life today? **DATE:** _____

Emotionally _____

Mentally _____

Physically _____

Spiritually _____

Socially _____

Courage Tools

What can I be thankful for?
Positivity _____

How do I say "stop," "no," "enough"?
Boundaries _____

Who do I need to forgive, including me?
Forgiveness _____

When or how can I confront this issue?
Confidence _____

What are the possibilities or opportunities?
Hope _____

Courage Challenge: What is something you can do or say differently today, which you have perhaps never done or done well before, that will challenge or change your broken pattern?

DATE: _____

How do you feel about yourself and your life today?

Emotionally _____

Mentally _____

Physically _____

Spiritually _____

Socially _____

Courage Tools

What can I be thankful for?
Positivity _____

How do I say "stop," "no," "enough"?
Boundaries _____

Who do I need to forgive, including me?
Forgiveness _____

When or how can I confront this issue?
Confidence _____

What are the possibilities or opportunities?
Hope _____

Courage Challenge: What is something you can do or say differently today, which you have perhaps never done or done well before, that will challenge or change your broken pattern?

How do you feel about yourself and your life today?   **DATE:** _____

Emotionally _____

Mentally   _____

Physically   _____

Spiritually _____

Socially   _____

Courage Tools

What can I be thankful for?
Positivity _____

How do I say "stop," "no," "enough"?
Boundaries _____

Who do I need to forgive, including me?
Forgiveness _____

When or how can I confront this issue?
Confidence _____

What are the possibilities or opportunities?
Hope _____

Courage Challenge: What is something you can do or say differently today, which you have perhaps never done or done well before, that will challenge or change your broken pattern?

How do you feel about yourself and your life today? **DATE:** _____

Emotionally _____

Mentally _____

Physically _____

Spiritually _____

Socially _____

Courage Tools

What can I be thankful for?
Positivity _____

How do I say "stop," "no," "enough"?
Boundaries _____

Who do I need to forgive, including me?
Forgiveness _____

When or how can I confront this issue?
Confidence _____

What are the possibilities or opportunities?
Hope _____

Courage Challenge: What is something you can do or say differently today, which you have perhaps never done or done well before, that will challenge or change your broken pattern?

How do you feel about yourself and your life today? **DATE:** _____

Emotionally _____

Mentally _____

Physically _____

Spiritually _____

Socially _____

Courage Tools

What can I be thankful for?
Positivity _____

How do I say "stop," "no," "enough"?
Boundaries _____

Who do I need to forgive, including me?
Forgiveness _____

When or how can I confront this issue?
Confidence _____

What are the possibilities or opportunities?
Hope _____

Courage Challenge: What is something you can do or say differently today, which you have perhaps never done or done well before, that will challenge or change your broken pattern?

From 1 to 10 with 10 being the best, how did you do this week with confronting, challenging or changing your broken patterns?

_____

Why did you do so well or so poorly?

_____

What is it going to take to get to the next level?

_____

How do you feel about yourself and your life today?   **DATE:** _____

Emotionally _____

Mentally _____

Physically _____

Spiritually _____

Socially _____

Courage Tools

What can I be thankful for?
Positivity _____

How do I say "stop," "no," "enough"?
Boundaries _____

Who do I need to forgive, including me?
Forgiveness _____

When or how can I confront this issue?
Confidence _____

What are the possibilities or opportunities?
Hope _____

Courage Challenge: What is something you can do or say differently today, which you have perhaps never done or done well before, that will challenge or change your broken pattern?

How do you feel about yourself and your life today? **DATE:** _____

Emotionally _____
Mentally _____
Physically _____
Spiritually _____
Socially _____

Courage Tools

What can I be thankful for?
Positivity _____

How do I say "stop," "no," "enough"?
Boundaries _____

Who do I need to forgive, including me?
Forgiveness _____

When or how can I confront this issue?
Confidence _____

What are the possibilities or opportunities?
Hope _____

Courage Challenge: What is something you can do or say differently today, which you have perhaps never done or done well before, that will challenge or change your broken pattern?

How do you feel about yourself and your life today? **DATE:** _____

Emotionally _____

Mentally _____

Physically _____

Spiritually _____

Socially _____

Courage Tools

What can I be thankful for?
Positivity _____

How do I say "stop," "no," "enough"?
Boundaries _____

Who do I need to forgive, including me?
Forgiveness _____

When or how can I confront this issue?
Confidence _____

What are the possibilities or opportunities?
Hope _____

Courage Challenge: What is something you can do or say differently today, which you have perhaps never done or done well before, that will challenge or change your broken pattern?

How do you feel about yourself and your life today?   **DATE:** _____

Emotionally _____

Mentally _____

Physically _____

Spiritually _____

Socially _____

Courage Tools

What can I be thankful for?
Positivity _____

How do I say "stop," "no," "enough"?
Boundaries _____

Who do I need to forgive, including me?
Forgiveness _____

When or how can I confront this issue?
Confidence _____

What are the possibilities or opportunities?
Hope _____

Courage Challenge: What is something you can do or say differently today, which you have perhaps never done or done well before, that will challenge or change your broken pattern?

How do you feel about yourself and your life today? **DATE:** _____

Emotionally _____

Mentally _____

Physically _____

Spiritually _____

Socially _____

Courage Tools

What can I be thankful for?
Positivity _____

How do I say "stop," "no," "enough"?
Boundaries _____

Who do I need to forgive, including me?
Forgiveness _____

When or how can I confront this issue?
Confidence _____

What are the possibilities or opportunities?
Hope _____

Courage Challenge: What is something you can do or say differently today, which you have perhaps never done or done well before, that will challenge or change your broken pattern?

How do you feel about yourself and your life today?   **DATE:** _____

Emotionally _____

Mentally   _____

Physically   _____

Spiritually _____

Socially   _____

Courage Tools

What can I be thankful for?
Positivity _____

How do I say "stop," "no," "enough"?
Boundaries _____

Who do I need to forgive, including me?
Forgiveness _____

When or how can I confront this issue?
Confidence _____

What are the possibilities or opportunities?
Hope _____

Courage Challenge: What is something you can do or say differently today, which you have perhaps never done or done well before, that will challenge or change your broken pattern?

How do you feel about yourself and your life today? **DATE:** _____

Emotionally _____

Mentally _____

Physically _____

Spiritually _____

Socially _____

Courage Tools

What can I be thankful for?
Positivity _____

How do I say "stop," "no," "enough"?
Boundaries _____

Who do I need to forgive, including me?
Forgiveness _____

When or how can I confront this issue?
Confidence _____

What are the possibilities or opportunities?
Hope _____

Courage Challenge: What is something you can do or say differently today, which you have perhaps never done or done well before, that will challenge or change your broken pattern?

Weekly
U P D A T E . .

From 1 to 10 with 10 being the best, how did you do this week with confronting, challenging or changing your broken patterns?

_____

Why did you do so well or so poorly?

_____

What is it going to take to get to the next level?

_____

> "Be faithful in small things because it is in them that your strength lies."

— MOTHER TERESA -

STRONGER DAYS

Because the first step to restoring your brokenness is admitting that you are broken, think about the aspect of your life that you most need to address this month:

_____

_____

_____

_____

_____

_____

_____

For the next several weeks, think about how you can confront and overcome your issue(s) by writing down your thoughts on the following pages each day.

How do you feel about yourself and your life today? **DATE:** _____

Emotionally _____

Mentally _____

Physically _____

Spiritually _____

Socially _____

Courage Tools

What can I be thankful for?
Positivity _____

How do I say "stop," "no," "enough"?
Boundaries _____

Who do I need to forgive, including me?
Forgiveness _____

When or how can I confront this issue?
Confidence _____

What are the possibilities or opportunities?
Hope _____

Courage Challenge: What is something you can do or say differently today, which you have perhaps never done or done well before, that will challenge or change your broken pattern?

How do you feel about yourself and your life today? **DATE:** _____

Emotionally _____

Mentally _____

Physically _____

Spiritually _____

Socially _____

Courage Tools

What can I be thankful for?
Positivity _____

How do I say "stop," "no," "enough"?
Boundaries _____

Who do I need to forgive, including me?
Forgiveness _____

When or how can I confront this issue?
Confidence _____

What are the possibilities or opportunities?
Hope _____

Courage Challenge: What is something you can do or say differently today, which you have perhaps never done or done well before, that will challenge or change your broken pattern?

How do you feel about yourself and your life today? **DATE:** _____

Emotionally _____

Mentally _____

Physically _____

Spiritually _____

Socially _____

Courage Tools

What can I be thankful for?
Positivity _____

How do I say "stop," "no," "enough"?
Boundaries _____

Who do I need to forgive, including me?
Forgiveness _____

When or how can I confront this issue?
Confidence _____

What are the possibilities or opportunities?
Hope _____

Courage Challenge: What is something you can do or say differently today, which you have perhaps never done or done well before, that will challenge or change your broken pattern?

How do you feel about yourself and your life today?   **DATE:** _____

Emotionally   _____

Mentally   _____

Physically   _____

Spiritually   _____

Socially   _____

Courage Tools

What can I be thankful for?
Positivity _____

How do I say "stop," "no," "enough"?
Boundaries _____

Who do I need to forgive, including me?
Forgiveness _____

When or how can I confront this issue?
Confidence _____

What are the possibilities or opportunities?
Hope _____

Courage Challenge: What is something you can do or say differently today, which you have perhaps never done or done well before, that will challenge or change your broken pattern?

How do you feel about yourself and your life today? **DATE:** _____

Emotionally _____

Mentally _____

Physically _____

Spiritually _____

Socially _____

Courage Tools

What can I be thankful for?
Positivity _____

How do I say "stop," "no," "enough"?
Boundaries _____

Who do I need to forgive, including me?
Forgiveness _____

When or how can I confront this issue?
Confidence _____

What are the possibilities or opportunities?
Hope _____

Courage Challenge: What is something you can do or say differently today, which you have perhaps never done or done well before, that will challenge or change your broken pattern?

How do you feel about yourself and your life today?   **DATE:** _____

Emotionally   _____

Mentally   _____

Physically   _____

Spiritually   _____

Socially   _____

Courage Tools

What can I be thankful for?
Positivity _____

How do I say "stop," "no," "enough"?
Boundaries _____

Who do I need to forgive, including me?
Forgiveness _____

When or how can I confront this issue?
Confidence _____

What are the possibilities or opportunities?
Hope _____

Courage Challenge: What is something you can do or say differently today, which you have perhaps never done or done well before, that will challenge or change your broken pattern?

How do you feel about yourself and your life today?   **DATE:** _____

Emotionally   _____

Mentally   _____

Physically   _____

Spiritually   _____

Socially   _____

Courage Tools

What can I be thankful for?
Positivity _____

How do I say "stop," "no," "enough"?
Boundaries _____

Who do I need to forgive, including me?
Forgiveness _____

When or how can I confront this issue?
Confidence _____

What are the possibilities or opportunities?
Hope _____

Courage Challenge: What is something you can do or say differently today, which you have perhaps never done or done well before, that will challenge or change your broken pattern?

Weekly
U P D A T E . .

From 1 to 10 with 10 being the best, how did you do this week with confronting, challenging or changing your broken patterns?

_____

Why did you do so well or so poorly?

_____

What is it going to take to get to the next level?

_____

How do you feel about yourself and your life today?   **DATE:** _____

Emotionally _____

Mentally _____

Physically _____

Spiritually _____

Socially _____

Courage Tools

What can I be thankful for?
Positivity _____

How do I say "stop," "no," "enough"?
Boundaries _____

Who do I need to forgive, including me?
Forgiveness _____

When or how can I confront this issue?
Confidence _____

What are the possibilities or opportunities?
Hope _____

Courage Challenge: What is something you can do or say differently today, which you have perhaps never done or done well before, that will challenge or change your broken pattern?

How do you feel about yourself and your life today?   **DATE:** _____

Emotionally _____

Mentally   _____

Physically   _____

Spiritually _____

Socially   _____

Courage Tools

What can I be thankful for?
Positivity _____

How do I say "stop," "no," "enough"?
Boundaries _____

Who do I need to forgive, including me?
Forgiveness _____

When or how can I confront this issue?
Confidence _____

What are the possibilities or opportunities?
Hope _____

Courage Challenge: What is something you can do or say differently today, which you have perhaps never done or done well before, that will challenge or change your broken pattern?

How do you feel about yourself and your life today? **DATE:** _____

Emotionally _____

Mentally _____

Physically _____

Spiritually _____

Socially _____

Courage Tools

What can I be thankful for?
Positivity _____

How do I say "stop," "no," "enough"?
Boundaries _____

Who do I need to forgive, including me?
Forgiveness _____

When or how can I confront this issue?
Confidence _____

What are the possibilities or opportunities?
Hope _____

Courage Challenge: What is something you can do or say differently today, which you have perhaps never done or done well before, that will challenge or change your broken pattern?

How do you feel about yourself and your life today? **DATE:** _____

Emotionally _____

Mentally _____

Physically _____

Spiritually _____

Socially _____

Courage Tools

What can I be thankful for?
Positivity _____

How do I say "stop," "no," "enough"?
Boundaries _____

Who do I need to forgive, including me?
Forgiveness _____

When or how can I confront this issue?
Confidence _____

What are the possibilities or opportunities?
Hope _____

Courage Challenge: What is something you can do or say differently today, which you have perhaps never done or done well before, that will challenge or change your broken pattern?

How do you feel about yourself and your life today?   **DATE:** _____

Emotionally _____

Mentally   _____

Physically   _____

Spiritually _____

Socially   _____

Courage Tools

What can I be thankful for?
Positivity _____

How do I say "stop," "no," "enough"?
Boundaries _____

Who do I need to forgive, including me?
Forgiveness _____

When or how can I confront this issue?
Confidence _____

What are the possibilities or opportunities?
Hope _____

Courage Challenge: What is something you can do or say differently today, which you have perhaps never done or done well before, that will challenge or change your broken pattern?

How do you feel about yourself and your life today?   **DATE:** _____

Emotionally _____

Mentally _____

Physically _____

Spiritually _____

Socially _____

Courage Tools

What can I be thankful for?
Positivity _____

How do I say "stop," "no," "enough"?
Boundaries _____

Who do I need to forgive, including me?
Forgiveness _____

When or how can I confront this issue?
Confidence _____

What are the possibilities or opportunities?
Hope _____

Courage Challenge: What is something you can do or say differently today, which you have perhaps never done or done well before, that will challenge or change your broken pattern?

How do you feel about yourself and your life today?   **DATE:** _____

Emotionally _____

Mentally   _____

Physically   _____

Spiritually   _____

Socially   _____

Courage Tools

What can I be thankful for?
Positivity _____

How do I say "stop," "no," "enough"?
Boundaries _____

Who do I need to forgive, including me?
Forgiveness _____

When or how can I confront this issue?
Confidence _____

What are the possibilities or opportunities?
Hope _____

Courage Challenge: What is something you can do or say differently today, which you have perhaps never done or done well before, that will challenge or change your broken pattern?

Weekly
U P D A T E . .

From 1 to 10 with 10 being the best, how did you do this week with confronting, challenging or changing your broken patterns?

_____

Why did you do so well or so poorly?

_____

What is it going to take to get to the next level?

_____

How do you feel about yourself and your life today? **DATE:** _____

Emotionally _____

Mentally _____

Physically _____

Spiritually _____

Socially _____

Courage Tools

What can I be thankful for?
Positivity _____

How do I say "stop," "no," "enough"?
Boundaries _____

Who do I need to forgive, including me?
Forgiveness _____

When or how can I confront this issue?
Confidence _____

What are the possibilities or opportunities?
Hope _____

Courage Challenge: What is something you can do or say differently today, which you have perhaps never done or done well before, that will challenge or change your broken pattern?

How do you feel about yourself and your life today? **DATE:** _____

Emotionally _____

Mentally _____

Physically _____

Spiritually _____

Socially _____

Courage Tools

What can I be thankful for?
Positivity _____

How do I say "stop," "no," "enough"?
Boundaries _____

Who do I need to forgive, including me?
Forgiveness _____

When or how can I confront this issue?
Confidence _____

What are the possibilities or opportunities?
Hope _____

Courage Challenge: What is something you can do or say differently today, which you have perhaps never done or done well before, that will challenge or change your broken pattern?

How do you feel about yourself and your life today?   **DATE:** _____

Emotionally _____
Mentally _____
Physically _____
Spiritually _____
Socially _____

Courage Tools

What can I be thankful for?
Positivity _____

How do I say "stop," "no," "enough"?
Boundaries _____

Who do I need to forgive, including me?
Forgiveness _____

When or how can I confront this issue?
Confidence _____

What are the possibilities or opportunities?
Hope _____

Courage Challenge: What is something you can do or say differently today, which you have perhaps never done or done well before, that will challenge or change your broken pattern?

How do you feel about yourself and your life today?   **DATE:** _____

Emotionally   _____

Mentally   _____

Physically   _____

Spiritually   _____

Socially   _____

Courage Tools

What can I be thankful for?
Positivity _____

How do I say "stop," "no," "enough"?
Boundaries _____

Who do I need to forgive, including me?
Forgiveness _____

When or how can I confront this issue?
Confidence _____

What are the possibilities or opportunities?
Hope _____

Courage Challenge: What is something you can do or say differently today, which you have perhaps never done or done well before, that will challenge or change your broken pattern?

How do you feel about yourself and your life today?   **DATE:** _____

Emotionally   _____

Mentally   _____

Physically   _____

Spiritually   _____

Socially   _____

Courage Tools

What can I be thankful for?
Positivity _____

How do I say "stop," "no," "enough"?
Boundaries _____

Who do I need to forgive, including me?
Forgiveness _____

When or how can I confront this issue?
Confidence _____

What are the possibilities or opportunities?
Hope _____

Courage Challenge: What is something you can do or say differently today, which you have perhaps never done or done well before, that will challenge or change your broken pattern?

How do you feel about yourself and your life today?   **DATE:** _____

Emotionally   _____

Mentally   _____

Physically   _____

Spiritually   _____

Socially   _____

Courage Tools

What can I be thankful for?
Positivity _____

How do I say "stop," "no," "enough"?
Boundaries _____

Who do I need to forgive, including me?
Forgiveness _____

When or how can I confront this issue?
Confidence _____

What are the possibilities or opportunities?
Hope _____

Courage Challenge: What is something you can do or say differently today, which you have perhaps never done or done well before, that will challenge or change your broken pattern?

How do you feel about yourself and your life today?   **DATE:** _____

Emotionally _____

Mentally _____

Physically _____

Spiritually _____

Socially _____

Courage Tools

What can I be thankful for?
Positivity _____

How do I say "stop," "no," "enough"?
Boundaries _____

Who do I need to forgive, including me?
Forgiveness _____

When or how can I confront this issue?
Confidence _____

What are the possibilities or opportunities?
Hope _____

Courage Challenge: What is something you can do or say differently today, which you have perhaps never done or done well before, that will challenge or change your broken pattern?

Weekly
UPDATE..

From 1 to 10 with 10 being the best, how did you do this week with confronting, challenging or changing your broken patterns?

_____

Why did you do so well or so poorly?

_____

What is it going to take to get to the next level?

_____

How do you feel about yourself and your life today? **DATE:** _____

Emotionally _____

Mentally _____

Physically _____

Spiritually _____

Socially _____

Courage Tools

What can I be thankful for?
Positivity _____

How do I say "stop," "no," "enough"?
Boundaries _____

Who do I need to forgive, including me?
Forgiveness _____

When or how can I confront this issue?
Confidence _____

What are the possibilities or opportunities?
Hope _____

Courage Challenge: What is something you can do or say differently today, which you have perhaps never done or done well before, that will challenge or change your broken pattern?

DATE:

How do you feel about yourself and your life today?

Emotionally _____

Mentally _____

Physically _____

Spiritually _____

Socially _____

Courage Tools

What can I be thankful for?
Positivity _____

How do I say "stop," "no," "enough"?
Boundaries _____

Who do I need to forgive, including me?
Forgiveness _____

When or how can I confront this issue?
Confidence _____

What are the possibilities or opportunities?
Hope _____

Courage Challenge: What is something you can do or say differently today, which you have perhaps never done or done well before, that will challenge or change your broken pattern?

How do you feel about yourself and your life today? **DATE:** _____

Emotionally _____

Mentally _____

Physically _____

Spiritually _____

Socially _____

Courage Tools

What can I be thankful for?
Positivity _____

How do I say "stop," "no," "enough"?
Boundaries _____

Who do I need to forgive, including me?
Forgiveness _____

When or how can I confront this issue?
Confidence _____

What are the possibilities or opportunities?
Hope _____

Courage Challenge: What is something you can do or say differently today, which you have perhaps never done or done well before, that will challenge or change your broken pattern?

How do you feel about yourself and your life today? **DATE:** _____

Emotionally _____

Mentally _____

Physically _____

Spiritually _____

Socially _____

Courage Tools

What can I be thankful for?
Positivity _____

How do I say "stop," "no," "enough"?
Boundaries _____

Who do I need to forgive, including me?
Forgiveness _____

When or how can I confront this issue?
Confidence _____

What are the possibilities or opportunities?
Hope _____

Courage Challenge: What is something you can do or say differently today, which you have perhaps never done or done well before, that will challenge or change your broken pattern?

How do you feel about yourself and your life today? **DATE:** _____

Emotionally _____

Mentally _____

Physically _____

Spiritually _____

Socially _____

Courage Tools

What can I be thankful for?
Positivity _____

How do I say "stop," "no," "enough"?
Boundaries _____

Who do I need to forgive, including me?
Forgiveness _____

When or how can I confront this issue?
Confidence _____

What are the possibilities or opportunities?
Hope _____

Courage Challenge: What is something you can do or say differently today, which you have perhaps never done or done well before, that will challenge or change your broken pattern?

How do you feel about yourself and your life today? **DATE:** _____

Emotionally _____

Mentally _____

Physically _____

Spiritually _____

Socially _____

Courage Tools

What can I be thankful for?
Positivity _____

How do I say "stop," "no," "enough"?
Boundaries _____

Who do I need to forgive, including me?
Forgiveness _____

When or how can I confront this issue?
Confidence _____

What are the possibilities or opportunities?
Hope _____

Courage Challenge: What is something you can do or say differently today, which you have perhaps never done or done well before, that will challenge or change your broken pattern?

How do you feel about yourself and your life today?   **DATE:** _____

Emotionally _____

Mentally _____

Physically _____

Spiritually _____

Socially _____

Courage Tools

What can I be thankful for?
Positivity _____

How do I say "stop," "no," "enough"?
Boundaries _____

Who do I need to forgive, including me?
Forgiveness _____

When or how can I confront this issue?
Confidence _____

What are the possibilities or opportunities?
Hope _____

Courage Challenge: What is something you can do or say differently today, which you have perhaps never done or done well before, that will challenge or change your broken pattern?

Weekly
U P D A T E . .

From 1 to 10 with 10 being the best, how did you do this week with confronting, challenging or changing your broken patterns?

_____

Why did you do so well or so poorly?

_____

What is it going to take to get to the next level?

_____

> "Be strong and courageous. Do not be afraid or terrified because of them, for the Lord your God goes with you; he will never leave you nor forsake you."

— DEUTERONOMY 31:6 —

STRONGER DAYS

Because the first step to restoring your brokenness is admitting that you are broken, think about the aspect of your life that you most need to address this month:

_____

_____

_____

_____

_____

_____

_____

For the next several weeks, think about how you can confront and overcome your issue(s) by writing down your thoughts on the following pages each day.

How do you feel about yourself and your life today? **DATE:** _____

Emotionally _____

Mentally _____

Physically _____

Spiritually _____

Socially _____

Courage Tools

What can I be thankful for?
Positivity _____

How do I say "stop," "no," "enough"?
Boundaries _____

Who do I need to forgive, including me?
Forgiveness _____

When or how can I confront this issue?
Confidence _____

What are the possibilities or opportunities?
Hope _____

Courage Challenge: What is something you can do or say differently today, which you have perhaps never done or done well before, that will challenge or change your broken pattern?

How do you feel about yourself and your life today? **DATE:** _____

Emotionally _____
Mentally _____
Physically _____
Spiritually _____
Socially _____

Courage Tools

What can I be thankful for?
Positivity _____

How do I say "stop," "no," "enough"?
Boundaries _____

Who do I need to forgive, including me?
Forgiveness _____

When or how can I confront this issue?
Confidence _____

What are the possibilities or opportunities?
Hope _____

Courage Challenge: What is something you can do or say differently today, which you have perhaps never done or done well before, that will challenge or change your broken pattern?

How do you feel about yourself and your life today?   **DATE:** _____

Emotionally _____

Mentally _____

Physically _____

Spiritually _____

Socially _____

Courage Tools

What can I be thankful for?
Positivity _____

How do I say "stop," "no," "enough"?
Boundaries _____

Who do I need to forgive, including me?
Forgiveness _____

When or how can I confront this issue?
Confidence _____

What are the possibilities or opportunities?
Hope _____

Courage Challenge: What is something you can do or say differently today, which you have perhaps never done or done well before, that will challenge or change your broken pattern?

How do you feel about yourself and your life today?   **DATE:** _____

Emotionally _____

Mentally   _____

Physically   _____

Spiritually _____

Socially   _____

Courage Tools

What can I be thankful for?
Positivity _____

How do I say "stop," "no," "enough"?
Boundaries _____

Who do I need to forgive, including me?
Forgiveness _____

When or how can I confront this issue?
Confidence _____

What are the possibilities or opportunities?
Hope _____

Courage Challenge: What is something you can do or say differently today, which you have perhaps never done or done well before, that will challenge or change your broken pattern?

How do you feel about yourself and your life today?   **DATE:** _____

Emotionally _____

Mentally _____

Physically _____

Spiritually _____

Socially _____

Courage Tools

What can I be thankful for?
Positivity _____

How do I say "stop," "no," "enough"?
Boundaries _____

Who do I need to forgive, including me?
Forgiveness _____

When or how can I confront this issue?
Confidence _____

What are the possibilities or opportunities?
Hope _____

Courage Challenge: What is something you can do or say differently today, which you have perhaps never done or done well before, that will challenge or change your broken pattern?

How do you feel about yourself and your life today? **DATE:** _____

Emotionally _____

Mentally _____

Physically _____

Spiritually _____

Socially _____

Courage Tools

What can I be thankful for?
Positivity _____

How do I say "stop," "no," "enough"?
Boundaries _____

Who do I need to forgive, including me?
Forgiveness _____

When or how can I confront this issue?
Confidence _____

What are the possibilities or opportunities?
Hope _____

Courage Challenge: What is something you can do or say differently today, which you have perhaps never done or done well before, that will challenge or change your broken pattern?

How do you feel about yourself and your life today?   **DATE:** _____

Emotionally   _____

Mentally   _____

Physically   _____

Spiritually   _____

Socially   _____

Courage Tools

What can I be thankful for?
Positivity _____

How do I say "stop," "no," "enough"?
Boundaries _____

Who do I need to forgive, including me?
Forgiveness _____

When or how can I confront this issue?
Confidence _____

What are the possibilities or opportunities?
Hope _____

Courage Challenge: What is something you can do or say differently today, which you have perhaps never done or done well before, that will challenge or change your broken pattern?

Weekly
U P D A T E . .

From 1 to 10 with 10 being the best, how did you do this week with confronting, challenging or changing your broken patterns?

_____

Why did you do so well or so poorly?

_____

What is it going to take to get to the next level?

_____

How do you feel about yourself and your life today? **DATE:** _____

Emotionally _____

Mentally _____

Physically _____

Spiritually _____

Socially _____

Courage Tools

What can I be thankful for?
Positivity _____

How do I say "stop," "no," "enough"?
Boundaries _____

Who do I need to forgive, including me?
Forgiveness _____

When or how can I confront this issue?
Confidence _____

What are the possibilities or opportunities?
Hope _____

Courage Challenge: What is something you can do or say differently today, which you have perhaps never done or done well before, that will challenge or change your broken pattern?

How do you feel about yourself and your life today?   **DATE:** _____

Emotionally   _____

Mentally   _____

Physically   _____

Spiritually   _____

Socially   _____

Courage Tools

What can I be thankful for?
Positivity _____

How do I say "stop," "no," "enough"?
Boundaries _____

Who do I need to forgive, including me?
Forgiveness _____

When or how can I confront this issue?
Confidence _____

What are the possibilities or opportunities?
Hope _____

Courage Challenge: What is something you can do or say differently today, which you have perhaps never done or done well before, that will challenge or change your broken pattern?

How do you feel about yourself and your life today? **DATE:** _____

Emotionally _____

Mentally _____

Physically _____

Spiritually _____

Socially _____

Courage Tools

What can I be thankful for?
Positivity _____

How do I say "stop," "no," "enough"?
Boundaries _____

Who do I need to forgive, including me?
Forgiveness _____

When or how can I confront this issue?
Confidence _____

What are the possibilities or opportunities?
Hope _____

Courage Challenge: What is something you can do or say differently today, which you have perhaps never done or done well before, that will challenge or change your broken pattern?

How do you feel about yourself and your life today?

DATE: _____

Emotionally _____

Mentally _____

Physically _____

Spiritually _____

Socially _____

Courage Tools

What can I be thankful for?
Positivity _____

How do I say "stop," "no," "enough"?
Boundaries _____

Who do I need to forgive, including me?
Forgiveness _____

When or how can I confront this issue?
Confidence _____

What are the possibilities or opportunities?
Hope _____

Courage Challenge: What is something you can do or say differently today, which you have perhaps never done or done well before, that will challenge or change your broken pattern?

How do you feel about yourself and your life today?   **DATE:** _____

Emotionally _____

Mentally   _____

Physically   _____

Spiritually _____

Socially   _____

Courage Tools

What can I be thankful for?
Positivity _____

How do I say "stop," "no," "enough"?
Boundaries _____

Who do I need to forgive, including me?
Forgiveness _____

When or how can I confront this issue?
Confidence _____

What are the possibilities or opportunities?
Hope _____

Courage Challenge: What is something you can do or say differently today, which you have perhaps never done or done well before, that will challenge or change your broken pattern?

How do you feel about yourself and your life today?   **DATE:** _____

Emotionally   _____

Mentally   _____

Physically   _____

Spiritually   _____

Socially   _____

Courage Tools

What can I be thankful for?
Positivity _____

How do I say "stop," "no," "enough"?
Boundaries _____

Who do I need to forgive, including me?
Forgiveness _____

When or how can I confront this issue?
Confidence _____

What are the possibilities or opportunities?
Hope _____

Courage Challenge: What is something you can do or say differently today, which you have perhaps never done or done well before, that will challenge or change your broken pattern?

How do you feel about yourself and your life today? **DATE:** _____

Emotionally _____

Mentally _____

Physically _____

Spiritually _____

Socially _____

Courage Tools

What can I be thankful for?
Positivity _____

How do I say "stop," "no," "enough"?
Boundaries _____

Who do I need to forgive, including me?
Forgiveness _____

When or how can I confront this issue?
Confidence _____

What are the possibilities or opportunities?
Hope _____

Courage Challenge: What is something you can do or say differently today, which you have perhaps never done or done well before, that will challenge or change your broken pattern?

Weekly
UPDATE..

From 1 to 10 with 10 being the best, how did you do this week with confronting, challenging or changing your broken patterns?

_____

Why did you do so well or so poorly?

_____

What is it going to take to get to the next level?

_____

How do you feel about yourself and your life today?   **DATE:** _____

Emotionally   _____

Mentally   _____

Physically   _____

Spiritually   _____

Socially   _____

Courage Tools

What can I be thankful for?
Positivity _____

How do I say "stop," "no," "enough"?
Boundaries _____

Who do I need to forgive, including me?
Forgiveness _____

When or how can I confront this issue?
Confidence _____

What are the possibilities or opportunities?
Hope _____

Courage Challenge: What is something you can do or say differently today, which you have perhaps never done or done well before, that will challenge or change your broken pattern?

How do you feel about yourself and your life today? **DATE:** _____

Emotionally _____

Mentally _____

Physically _____

Spiritually _____

Socially _____

Courage Tools

What can I be thankful for?
Positivity _____

How do I say "stop," "no," "enough"?
Boundaries _____

Who do I need to forgive, including me?
Forgiveness _____

When or how can I confront this issue?
Confidence _____

What are the possibilities or opportunities?
Hope _____

Courage Challenge: What is something you can do or say differently today, which you have perhaps never done or done well before, that will challenge or change your broken pattern?

How do you feel about yourself and your life today? **DATE:** _____

Emotionally _____

Mentally _____

Physically _____

Spiritually _____

Socially _____

Courage Tools

What can I be thankful for?
Positivity _____

How do I say "stop," "no," "enough"?
Boundaries _____

Who do I need to forgive, including me?
Forgiveness _____

When or how can I confront this issue?
Confidence _____

What are the possibilities or opportunities?
Hope _____

Courage Challenge: What is something you can do or say differently today, which you have perhaps never done or done well before, that will challenge or change your broken pattern?

How do you feel about yourself and your life today?   **DATE:** _____

Emotionally   _____

Mentally   _____

Physically   _____

Spiritually   _____

Socially   _____

Courage Tools

What can I be thankful for?
Positivity _____

How do I say "stop," "no," "enough"?
Boundaries _____

Who do I need to forgive, including me?
Forgiveness _____

When or how can I confront this issue?
Confidence _____

What are the possibilities or opportunities?
Hope _____

Courage Challenge: What is something you can do or say differently today, which you have perhaps never done or done well before, that will challenge or change your broken pattern?

How do you feel about yourself and your life today? **DATE:** _____

Emotionally _____

Mentally _____

Physically _____

Spiritually _____

Socially _____

Courage Tools

What can I be thankful for?
Positivity _____

How do I say "stop," "no," "enough"?
Boundaries _____

Who do I need to forgive, including me?
Forgiveness _____

When or how can I confront this issue?
Confidence _____

What are the possibilities or opportunities?
Hope _____

Courage Challenge: What is something you can do or say differently today, which you have perhaps never done or done well before, that will challenge or change your broken pattern?

How do you feel about yourself and your life today? **DATE:** _____

Emotionally _____
Mentally   _____
Physically   _____
Spiritually _____
Socially   _____

Courage Tools

What can I be thankful for?
Positivity _____

How do I say "stop," "no," "enough"?
Boundaries _____

Who do I need to forgive, including me?
Forgiveness _____

When or how can I confront this issue?
Confidence _____

What are the possibilities or opportunities?
Hope _____

Courage Challenge: What is something you can do or say differently today, which you have perhaps never done or done well before, that will challenge or change your broken pattern?

How do you feel about yourself and your life today? **DATE:** _____

Emotionally _____

Mentally _____

Physically _____

Spiritually _____

Socially _____

Courage Tools

What can I be thankful for?
Positivity _____

How do I say "stop," "no," "enough"?
Boundaries _____

Who do I need to forgive, including me?
Forgiveness _____

When or how can I confront this issue?
Confidence _____

What are the possibilities or opportunities?
Hope _____

Courage Challenge: What is something you can do or say differently today, which you have perhaps never done or done well before, that will challenge or change your broken pattern?

Weekly
U P D A T E . .

From 1 to 10 with 10 being the best, how did you do this week with confronting, challenging or changing your broken patterns?

_____

Why did you do so well or so poorly?

_____

What is it going to take to get to the next level?

_____

How do you feel about yourself and your life today?   **DATE:** _____

Emotionally _____

Mentally _____

Physically _____

Spiritually _____

Socially _____

Courage Tools

What can I be thankful for?
Positivity _____

How do I say "stop," "no," "enough"?
Boundaries _____

Who do I need to forgive, including me?
Forgiveness _____

When or how can I confront this issue?
Confidence _____

What are the possibilities or opportunities?
Hope _____

Courage Challenge: What is something you can do or say differently today, which you have perhaps never done or done well before, that will challenge or change your broken pattern?

How do you feel about yourself and your life today? **DATE:** _____

Emotionally _____

Mentally _____

Physically _____

Spiritually _____

Socially _____

Courage Tools

What can I be thankful for?
Positivity _____

How do I say "stop," "no," "enough"?
Boundaries _____

Who do I need to forgive, including me?
Forgiveness _____

When or how can I confront this issue?
Confidence _____

What are the possibilities or opportunities?
Hope _____

Courage Challenge: What is something you can do or say differently today, which you have perhaps never done or done well before, that will challenge or change your broken pattern?

How do you feel about yourself and your life today?   **DATE:** _____

Emotionally _____

Mentally _____

Physically _____

Spiritually _____

Socially _____

Courage Tools

What can I be thankful for?
Positivity _____

How do I say "stop," "no," "enough"?
Boundaries _____

Who do I need to forgive, including me?
Forgiveness _____

When or how can I confront this issue?
Confidence _____

What are the possibilities or opportunities?
Hope _____

Courage Challenge: What is something you can do or say differently today, which you have perhaps never done or done well before, that will challenge or change your broken pattern?

How do you feel about yourself and your life today? **DATE:** _____

Emotionally _____

Mentally _____

Physically _____

Spiritually _____

Socially _____

Courage Tools

What can I be thankful for?
Positivity _____

How do I say "stop," "no," "enough"?
Boundaries _____

Who do I need to forgive, including me?
Forgiveness _____

When or how can I confront this issue?
Confidence _____

What are the possibilities or opportunities?
Hope _____

Courage Challenge: What is something you can do or say differently today, which you have perhaps never done or done well before, that will challenge or change your broken pattern?

How do you feel about yourself and your life today?   **DATE:** _____

Emotionally _____

Mentally   _____

Physically   _____

Spiritually _____

Socially   _____

Courage Tools

What can I be thankful for?
Positivity _____

How do I say "stop," "no," "enough"?
Boundaries _____

Who do I need to forgive, including me?
Forgiveness _____

When or how can I confront this issue?
Confidence _____

What are the possibilities or opportunities?
Hope _____

Courage Challenge: What is something you can do or say differently today, which you have perhaps never done or done well before, that will challenge or change your broken pattern?

How do you feel about yourself and your life today? **DATE:** _____

Emotionally _____
Mentally   _____
Physically   _____
Spiritually _____
Socially   _____

Courage Tools

What can I be thankful for?
Positivity _____

How do I say "stop," "no," "enough"?
Boundaries _____

Who do I need to forgive, including me?
Forgiveness _____

When or how can I confront this issue?
Confidence _____

What are the possibilities or opportunities?
Hope _____

Courage Challenge: What is something you can do or say differently today, which you have perhaps never done or done well before, that will challenge or change your broken pattern?

How do you feel about yourself and your life today?   **DATE:** _____

Emotionally _____

Mentally _____

Physically _____

Spiritually _____

Socially _____

Courage Tools

What can I be thankful for?
Positivity _____

How do I say "stop," "no," "enough"?
Boundaries _____

Who do I need to forgive, including me?
Forgiveness _____

When or how can I confront this issue?
Confidence _____

What are the possibilities or opportunities?
Hope _____

Courage Challenge: What is something you can do or say differently today, which you have perhaps never done or done well before, that will challenge or change your broken pattern?

UPDATE..

From 1 to 10 with 10 being the best, how did you do this week with confronting, challenging or changing your broken patterns?

_____

Why did you do so well or so poorly?

_____

What is it going to take to get to the next level?

_____

> "Be strong and take heart, all you who hope in the LORD."

— PSALM 31:24 —